CROWN & CLOISTER
The Royal Story of Westminster Abbey

CROWN & CLOISTER

The Royal Story of Westminster Abbey

James Wilkinson and C.S. Knighton

With an introduction by the Dean of Westminster

CONTENTS

The 450th anniversary of the granting of the Royal Charter to Westminster Abbey by Queen Elizabeth I is an occasion for both looking back with joy at the achievements over the years of this important institution and beautiful church, and for looking forward to its continuing importance in the future. The close association between the Crown and Westminster Abbey is one which reflects the special link between the Abbey and the life of the nation as a whole in the celebration and commemoration of many great moments in our history.

I send to the Dean and Chapter, and to all those who contribute to the varied work of the Abbey, my warm good wishes, and I pray that over the years to come Westminster Abbey may continue to reflect and inspire our national life, and to be a spiritual focus for people throughout Britain and the wider world.

ELIZABETH R.

INTRODUCTION

WESTMINSTER ABBEY is one of the great buildings of the world, with the Palace of Westminster judged by UNESCO to be part of the World Heritage. Every year well over a million visitors come to the Abbey from all over the world, many as tourists. We welcome them and hope their visit will develop in them a sense of wonder and that they will leave having experienced something of the worship of almighty God. In addition, thousands of people each week attend the acts of worship – Morning Prayer, the twice-daily Eucharist and Evensong – that provide the framework for the life of the Abbey.

The Abbey remains today what it has been from the beginning – a living church, above all a house of God, a place of Christian worship. The worship of God has been virtually unbroken throughout the Abbey's thousand-year history. Apart from the daily round of services, today's Abbey year includes many special acts of worship, often attended by members of the Royal Family, in commemoration and celebration, such as the annual Commonwealth Day Observance, ANZAC, Battle of Britain and Remembrance services, occasional services for special anniversaries, or to give thanks for the life of a distinguished citizen. Many special events relate to the 3,300 people, including statesmen, clergy, musicians, poets, scientists and actors, who are buried or memorialised in the Abbey.

As well as being a house of God, the Abbey is a house of kings. Edward the Confessor rebuilt the Abbey and was buried here in 1066. A hundred years later he was canonised as St Edward. On 13 October 1269, his body was translated to the shrine at the heart of Henry III's church, in which it remains. William the Conqueror was crowned here on Christmas Day 1066. Since then the coronation of every crowned monarch has taken place in the Abbey, most recently that of Her Majesty Queen Elizabeth II on 2 June 1953.

Royal ceremonials in the Abbey in the twentieth century have included the weddings of the Duke of York and Elizabeth Bowes-Lyon (later King George VI and Queen Elizabeth), of The Queen (then Princess Elizabeth) and the Duke of Edinburgh in 1947, of Princess Margaret, Princess Alexandra, Princess Anne and Prince Andrew. Many royal funerals have taken place in the Abbey, of which the most recent have been those of Diana, Princess of Wales, and Queen Elizabeth The Queen Mother. Most kings and queens were buried here until 1760. One king was born at the Abbey, another died here.

Westminster Abbey has enjoyed the patronage and active interest of successive kings and queens of England and of the United Kingdom from the earliest days. Edward the Confessor built his palace beside the Abbey, a powerful symbol of the collaboration of Church and State: of the need of the State for the prayers of the Church and the values of the Christian Gospel, and of the Church for the active support of the State. Two centuries later Henry III, out of personal devotion to Edward the Confessor, personally invested huge sums in rebuilding the Abbey. Henry VII's additional investment in the early sixteenth century enabled the replacement of the thirteenth-century Lady Chapel with the glorious building we enjoy today. When Henry VIII dissolved the monastery in 1540, he made the Abbey a cathedral (which it remained until 1550) and allowed it to retain many of its estates. In the eighteenth century Parliament voted the funds for the building of the west towers. The Abbey's endowments were mostly lost in the nineteenth century through a series of retrospectively disastrous decisions to the benefit of the church commissioners. Royal patronage and personal generosity was revived in the twentieth century. From the 1970s, substantial conservation and restoration work, costing £25 million and including the cleaning of the Abbey, was undertaken through a Trust chaired for more than twenty years by the Duke of Edinburgh.

The educational work of the Abbey particularly benefited from royal patronage in the sixteenth century. Like every other monastery the Abbey was a place of education. After the dissolution, Henry VIII made provision for education to be continued. In 1560 the schoolmasters and forty scholars were incorporated by Elizabeth I in what is now known as Westminster School when she re-founded the Abbey as the Collegiate Church of St Peter in Westminster. The Head Master, Under Master and Master of the Queen's Scholars, as well as the forty Queen's Scholars themselves, form part of the Abbey's collegiate foundation. The Scholars have the unique duty of shouting at each coronation *Vivat Rex / Regina* (essentially meaning 'Long live the King / Queen'), words incorporated by Parry into his coronation setting of the Psalm *I was glad*. Although Westminster School was formally separated from the Dean and Chapter in 1868, the Dean of Westminster remains chairman of the governing body, which also includes two canons of Westminster, the Dean of Christ Church, Oxford and the Master of Trinity College, Cambridge.

Elizabeth I's establishment in 1560 was for a Dean and twelve canons (originally known as prebendaries), their number since reduced to five (in practice there are four). That provision, with the foundation of the Collegiate Church of St Peter, has given the Abbey its current constitution and, with Westminster School, its year of celebration of 450 years of the collegiate foundation in 2010.

The Abbey is full of Christian faith and godly vigour and thinks actively about its future development. There seems no good reason why in another 450 years the Abbey should not be celebrating its first fifteen centuries and still looking forward with eager anticipation to the good things God has in store.

THE VERY REVEREND DR JOHN HALL, *Dean of Westminster*

scanr incrauutr.
rale sci Edmardi

nitatr gaudenr angeli

1 ROYAL BEGINNINGS

WESTMINSTER ABBEY'S royal story dates with certainty back to the building of a great church by King Edward the Confessor in 1065. Yet the site had long been occupied by a religious community, and much earlier royal associations were once claimed. The Westminster monks thought that their origins could be traced back to Sebert, King of the East Saxons, who died in 616. So convinced were they that in the thirteenth century they moved Sebert's supposed remains to a place of honour south of the high altar. Over the centuries few serious historians gave much credence to the notion that this obscure ruler was Westminster Abbey's founder. This scepticism proved justified when, in 2003, archaeologists found what they believed to be King Sebert's tomb at Prittlewell in Essex.

History, however, only properly begins with the written record. Ostensibly the oldest of the title deeds now in the Abbey's muniments (archives) purports to be a grant made in 785 by the Mercian King Offa, giving land at Aldenham in Hertfordshire to 'the needy people of God' at Westminster. The charter itself is spurious; it was quite common in medieval times for monasteries to manufacture such documents if they did not happen to have genuine ones. The Westminster monks certainly held the land in question, and another King Offa (of Essex) may well have been among their early benefactors. Although Sebert's bones and Offa's charter are not what they were once claimed to be, they both testify to the importance that royalty has always occupied in the history of Westminster Abbey.

We can say more confidently that around 960 St Dunstan, then Bishop of London, brought twelve monks from Glastonbury to establish a new community at Westminster. Whatever church already existed there, it was absorbed into Dunstan's foundation, and the Benedictine Rule was then kept for 500 years. Dunstan himself soon became Archbishop of Canterbury, and in this capacity he crowned King Edgar at Bath Abbey in 973, a ceremony which set the pattern for subsequent coronations at Westminster. So although Edward the Confessor has traditionally been called Westminster Abbey's founder, he did not start from scratch. He nevertheless rebuilt the Abbey church on such a grand scale, and endowed the community so generously, that 1065 truly marks a new beginning.

Edward the Confessor was the son of Ethelred II and Emma, daughter of Duke Richard I of Normandy. Edward's path to the throne had not been smooth. During his childhood England was invaded by King Cnut of Denmark, and in 1013 the eight-year-old Edward had been sent to Normandy for safety. Cnut took the throne and was succeeded by two of his sons in turn. Only when the second of these died was Edward able to return to claim his inheritance.

The story goes that, in thanksgiving, the new King vowed to make a pilgrimage to St Peter's in Rome; but in view of the perils of the journey and continuing unrest at home, he was advised not to leave. Pope Leo IX released him from his vow on condition that he built or restored a church in honour of St Peter. Edward's eye settled on the small monastery of Westminster, which was dedicated to St Peter. According to an early account of the King's life, 'he ordered that out of the tithes of all his revenues a noble building should be started, which would be worthy of the chief apostle'.

Hitherto the monastery contained just a handful of monks. It was set in countryside outside London, close to the main channel of the River Thames, which was said to carry 'plentiful merchandise of every kind for use from the whole world'. It was therefore an ideal site for the palace that Edward planted alongside his Abbey. From these roots there developed links between the Abbey and the State, which consolidated over the centuries, and are today as close as ever.

The church that arose here, probably just to the east of the one it replaced, must have astonished onlookers by its splendour. It was the first church in England to be built in the Romanesque style, similar to Jumièges Abbey in Normandy, which Edward knew well from his exile. We know something of its appearance because, as well as appearing in contemporary written descriptions, it is shown in the Bayeux Tapestry. It had six double bays, a lantern tower over the crossing 'reaching up with spiralling stairs in artistic profusion', and a lead-covered wooden roof. Foundations of pillars have been discovered under the

OPPOSITE: Illuminated initial showing Edward the Confessor, from the fourteenth-century Litlyngton Missal in the Abbey Library.

† Eadweard cyng gret Leoffine b. 7 Eadwine eorl 7 ealle m... as on Stæffordscire

freondlice. 7 ic kyþe eow þ ic habbe ge unnan criste 7 sce petre into ...minstre ...land æt Pertune.

7 ælc þæra þinga þær þe þær inn to hefd on wuda 7 on felda mid fa... mid socne swa full 7 swa

forð swa hit me sylfan onhanda stod on eallan þingan · þan abbude ... leofan 7 þam gebroþran

þe binnan þam mynstre wuniad. 7 ic nylle nane men geþafian þ þa... æniz þæra þinga

þæt þe þær in to hyrd.

present church, which show that the Confessor's building was nearly as big.

Edward never lived to see his abbey finished. He had worshipped there at Christmas 1065, but was already on his deathbed when the church was consecrated three days later, on the feast of the Holy Innocents. He died on the fourth or fifth of January, and was buried on the sixth, in a vault before the high altar. In those days this was invariably at the far east end of a church, against the wall of the apse. An arc of stone now under the floor of the Confessor's Chapel is thought to be all that survives of the semicircular apse of Edward's church, so it seems likely that the original vault was beneath the present shrine. Investigation by ground-penetrating radar in 2005 suggested that the burial chamber was about 1.8 metres (6 feet) wide, its access shaft covered by a previously unexplained square of marble between the shrine and the high altar. Today the Saint's body rests in his shrine directly above the burial chamber.

So what manner of man and what sort of king was Edward called the Confessor? Contemporary and near-contemporary accounts cannot always be trusted, but according to one it seems he was a paragon. Of 'splendid' height, he had white hair, a long white beard, rosy

ABOVE: A writ of Edward the Confessor granting land at Perton in Staffordshire to Westminster Abbey, *c*.1065. This is one of only three known authentic examples of the Confessor's seal.

LEFT: A section of the Bayeux Tapestry showing Edward the Confessor's body being carried to the Abbey for burial in January 1066, with men putting the finishing touches to the building.

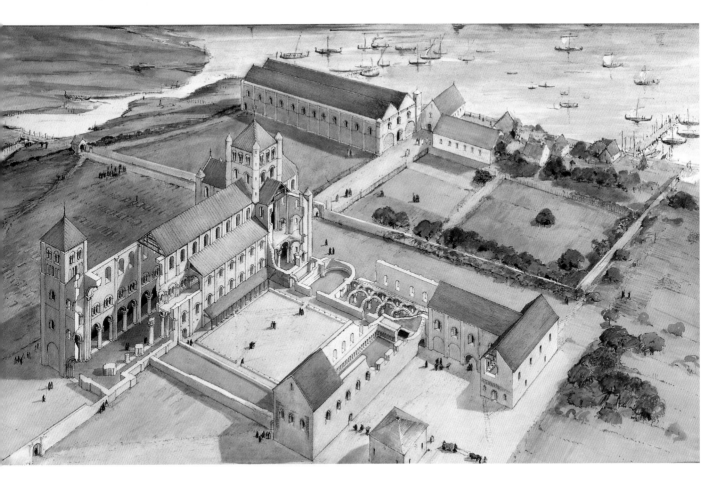

ABOVE: An artist's impression of the Abbey at the end of the eleventh century. The basic layout is little changed today.

cheeks and thin hands with long 'gleaming' fingers. He was dignified and agreeable. 'In public he conducted himself as a king and a lord, in private as a fellow among his own folk, albeit retaining his royal majesty.' Yet for all his virtues he was a timid and indecisive king, of no exceptional piety. It was left to successive biographers to praise his statesmanship, to invest him with increasingly holy powers, and to claim that during his lifetime he worked miracles that continued after his death. These stories were enthusiastically supported by the monks of Westminster. There was also the fact that Edward and his Queen, Edith, had no children, and it was suggested that their marriage was never consummated. Sexual abstinence was considered a mark of sanctity, so the King's reputation was enhanced further in the eyes of the Church.

Thirty-seven years after it had been closed, Edward's tomb was opened by Abbot Gilbert Crispin, with King Henry I looking on. To their surprise, Edward appeared to be simply asleep; his body had not deteriorated, and his joints were still flexible. The Bishop of Rochester tried to pluck a hair from the King's now yellowing beard, but was unable to do so. Uncorrupted remains were, and indeed still are, considered proof of holiness, so the campaign to have Edward formally declared a saint gained momentum. Though an initial attempt to secure canonisation failed, a further petition to Pope Alexander III in 1161 was successful. Two years later St Edward was moved, or translated, to a new shrine built by Henry II. The monks removed the cloth in which the body had been wrapped and made it into three copes; they also took Edward's ring and placed it with the Abbey's relics. Edward acquired the sobriquet of 'the Confessor' – a general term for saints not martyrs, applied in this case to distinguish the new Saint from his murdered uncle, King Edward the Martyr.

We know nothing of the original shrine because it was destroyed after a century, when Henry III rebuilt the Confessor's church in the Gothic style. A new and glorious shrine was then made, where the Saint's body was placed on the anniversary of its first removal, 13 October 1269. That day has ever since been kept as the feast of St Edward's translation, and the present Dean and Chapter has decided to give new emphasis to the celebration.

Edward the Confessor's chastity may have helped him into the kingdom of heaven, but it was calamitous for the old Saxon kingdom of England. As the childless King lay dying in the palace of Westminster, he named his brother-in-law Harold Godwinson as his successor, and Harold was duly crowned in 1066 on the day of the old King's funeral. Nevertheless, Edward had earlier promised the crown to his cousin Duke William of Normandy, who now determined to claim his right. William invaded England that year, and after Harold was killed at the battle of Hastings, took the throne. Two months later William was crowned in Westminster Abbey, choosing Christmas Day as an auspicious occasion on which to consolidate his hold on power. All did not go according to plan, however, and the ceremony nearly ended in disaster.

The Archbishop of Canterbury, Stigand, had refused to consecrate William because he was 'covered in the blood of men and the invader of others' rights'; so the Archbishop of York, Ealdred, officiated instead. William was crowned at the crossing of the church, on a stage elevated above head-height so that all might witness the event. Then, when the people were asked in French and in English whether they accepted William as their King, a roar of approval went up. This was heard and misunderstood by William's guards outside. Fearing a riot,

ABOVE: Scenes of Edward the Confessor's life from a thirteenth-century manuscript. He sees a vision of two pious monks; then, with Queen Edith at his side, he reports his experience.

BELOW: What is thought to be the oldest functioning door in Britain, now in the vestibule of the chapter house. It was made in the 1050s but much later was reduced in size to fit its present position.

they took revenge by setting fire to the surrounding buildings. The noise of the ensuing chaos alarmed those inside the Abbey, who panicked and fled, leaving the Conqueror apparently terrified.

The monks of Westminster can have had little to celebrate that Christmas Day, or on the first anniversary of their church's consecration three days later. Edward the Confessor's gifts of lands ensured that their community would be prosperous, but for long after his death the building work had to continue without further royal backing. Although William I had astutely used the Abbey to confer legitimacy on his regime, he had little further interest in the place. He took back for the Crown some of the land that Edward had given to the monks, including the manor of Windsor, where he built the castle that became royalty's favourite home and eventually gave William's descendants their family name. Westminster was compensated with other property and did rather well by the exchange. William added nothing to the fabric of the Abbey. In London his great legacy was a secular building – the castle later known as the White Tower, now part of the Tower of London. His religious foundations were elsewhere. He raised what is known as Battle Abbey on the site of his great victory, though he and his wife Matilda were buried back in Normandy, in the Abbey of St Stephen at Caen, which he had also built.

The Conqueror's second surviving son and successor in England, William II, similarly had little to do with Westminster Abbey. It is, however, to him that we owe another great building close by, Westminster Hall. The proximity of Abbey and Hall helped to make Westminster the ceremonial centre of the kingdom. William II was buried in Winchester Cathedral, near to the place where he met his death. The other Norman and early Plantagenet kings were all buried in churches they personally founded or favoured: Henry I at Reading, Stephen at Faversham, Henry II and Richard I at Fontevrault in Anjou, and John at Worcester. Only Henry II, in securing the Confessor's canonisation and building his shrine, left a significant mark at Westminster. It was to be John's son, Henry III, who would transform the Abbey in its entirety.

2 HENRY III'S GOTHIC ABBEY

DESPITE ITS MAGNIFICENCE, Edward the Confessor's church was not to last. In 1245 Henry III decided to replace it with an even more glorious building in the Gothic style, with soaring pointed arches and large windows. He was motivated mainly from increasing devotion to Edward, but he also wanted to indulge his developing interest in architecture and the arts, and to vie with the French in these areas.

Henry III succeeded his father in 1216 when he was only nine. He inherited a land that was riven by discord, but which had made its first faltering steps towards a sort of democracy when the barons forced King John to accept the terms of the Magna Carta. This placed the King under the law of the land and allowed the barons to impose sanctions on him if he broke it. Henry was first crowned in Gloucester Abbey (now the cathedral), since London was in hostile hands. He began to show his interest in building and the arts as a boy, and at the age of thirteen in 1220 he was already spending lavishly on his palace at Westminster. On 17 May that year he was crowned again, this time in the Abbey by Archbishop Stephen Langton. On the previous day Henry had laid the foundation stone of a new Lady Chapel, in which his interest steadily increased. Every aspect of its design claimed his attention, and he diverted men from work on his palace to help the construction. The monks, not surprisingly, encouraged his support.

It was not until 1232, when Henry was in his mid-twenties, that he began to rule in his own right. He was a man of peace, but that was a poor qualification for medieval kingship when he was expected to be a man of war. His kingdom was still repeatedly threatened by civil war, which he was desperate to avoid. As dissent increased, so did his devotion; he visited shrines and attended countless masses. When the French King told him he would do better to listen to sermons, Henry replied that he went to mass to meet the Lord, not to hear about him.

But why and when did Henry develop such esteem for Edward the Confessor? Part of the reason was increasing proximity. The thirteenth century saw the

OPPOSITE: The thirteenth-century Cosmati pavement, long hidden by a carpet, now competes for attention with the gilded Victorian reredos.

RIGHT: The original reredos or 'retable' of Henry III's high altar, now in the Abbey Museum. Though much damaged, its exquisite workmanship is evident from this detail showing Christ feeding the Five Thousand.

RIGHT: Behind the officiants' seats south of the high altar are paintings of two kings; this one could be Henry III, or perhaps Sebert.

end of the era of absentee kings. John had lost Normandy to the French in 1204, so after that the kings of England needed to spend much less time abroad. Though the Court was still on the road for most of the year, a more settled pattern evolved, and between 1235 and 1245 Henry spent more than a quarter of his time in Westminster. Previously Henry was rarely at the Abbey, yet from then on he was invariably in Westminster for the anniversaries of the Confessor's death and translation. We know this because letters and other documents he issued were copied on to rolls still preserved, each item ending with the date and the place where it was written. This evidence provides a detailed itinerary showing where Henry spent his days.

He also began to contribute to the Abbey's worship and furnishings. In 1238 he commissioned a tapestry to hang behind the high altar. He also gave precise instructions for the burning of candles in the church. His identification with St Edward extended to his private chamber, where the walls were decorated with scenes of the Saint's coronation and of the mythical story of his giving his ring to a beggar. Henry's devotion had practical advantages for the Westminster monks because in 1235 he issued a charter extending the Abbey's privileges. Four years later, in 1239, when his eldest son was born at Westminster, he named him Edward, after the Confessor.

Henry III's ambition to replace Edward's church may well have been driven by admiration for the architecture he had seen in France two years earlier. Louis IX had rebuilt the French coronation church, Reims Cathedral, and the Abbey of St Denis, where their kings were buried. Louis also erected the Sainte-Chapelle in Paris as a shrine for his most treasured possession, a relic of Christ's crown of thorns. Henry III wanted to combine these three functions in the Abbey at Westminster, and to rebuild it in the new style. The Abbey was already the coronation church, and it housed the tomb of one king, around which Henry intended his own tomb and those of his successors to be placed. The Abbey had also accumulated an impressive array of supposed relics, including such unlikely objects as a tooth of one of the Wise Men and a girdle belonging to the Virgin Mary. To

RIGHT: The central onyx roundel in the 700-year-old Cosmati pavement, which is made up of nearly 80,000 porphyry and glass tesserae. They are set in Purbeck marble.

this collection Henry gave further treasures, including a stone marked with the footprint of Christ himself. The most precious of these gifts was a phial of Christ's blood, which had been presented to Henry by the Patriarch of Jerusalem. The King carried it aloft to the Abbey in an elaborate procession, described by the chronicler Matthew Paris. Henry kept his eyes fixed on heaven or (more sensibly) on the container itself, when he came to an uneven section of the road. Having reached his destination without mishap, he presented 'this rich and priceless gift, which made all England illustrious, to God, to the church of St Peter at Westminster, to his beloved Edward and to the holy monks who minister there to God and his saints'.

Henry's building programme continued apace. Though it was inspired by French architecture, the interpretation was English. The French characteristics are most noticeable in the great height of the vault; at 31 metres (102 feet) it is the tallest in England, and its stunning impact is enhanced by the comparative narrowness of the aisles. There are cathedrals in France much loftier, yet none has the perfect proportions of Westminster Abbey.

Henry kept as many as 400 workmen labouring on the church during the summer months, including stone-cutters, masons, marblers, polishers, smiths, plumbers and glaziers. It was a massively expensive undertaking, costing five times what Henry's son Edward I later spent on each of his castles in Wales. Henry was keen to see his building progress as fast as possible, perhaps in part because he wanted to move the Saint's body into its new shrine in 1269, as in that year Easter Day would fall on the same date as in 1163, the year of the body's first translation. For the monks the building was a mixed blessing. They were being given a magnificent new church, but in the process their worship was confined to the nave, while constant noise and dust must have tried their patience.

Installed just behind the high altar was the focal point of the whole enterprise – the shrine, ready to receive the body of the Saint. Decked with precious stones and with a golden feretory above to contain the coffin, it shone like a beacon in the candlelight. It was elevated on a dais and had niches around the sides, where pilgrims could kneel and pray as close to the Saint as possible. At the west end was an altar, flanked by two pillars on which stood statues of St Edward himself and St John the Evangelist. The mosaic decoration of this chapel, and the pavement to the west of the high altar, was of a type new to England. Known as Cosmati work, it was imported from Rome, where Abbot Richard de Ware had seen examples when he visited Pope Alexander IV in 1258. So impressed was he that he invited the craftsmen to the Abbey. Part of their superb work (the pavement

in front of the high altar, long hidden by carpets) has recently been conserved and restored to give an impression of its pristine glory.

Throughout his reign, Henry continued to face opposition from the barons, and his building interests had to give way to affairs of state. Eventually the barons, frustrated by exclusion from power to which they felt entitled, provoked the civil war that Henry had so long feared, and took over the government. This constitutional struggle helped to develop Parliament, and the Abbey had an important place in its early history. From at least 1257 secular assemblies were occasionally held in the magnificent chapter house, which Henry III had built for the monks' deliberations. Later, after the local representatives first summoned in Henry III's reign had evolved into the House of Commons, their meetings often took place in the chapter house or the monks' refectory. Eventually the Commons were given a place of their own in the Palace of Westminster, and adopted St Margaret's, rather than the Abbey, as their church. Nevertheless the enduring bonds between the Abbey and Parliament owe much to their shared occupancy of Henry III's buildings.

By 1269 the quire and eastern part of the nave were finished, the new shrine was ready on schedule to receive the Confessor's body, and the church could be consecrated. The first part of Henry III's ambitious programme had been completed. Three years later the King died. With the Confessor's vault beneath the shrine now empty, Henry's own body was placed in it as a temporary measure. Although the new King, Edward I, commissioned a permanent tomb for his father, he did not share his larger vision for the new church. Once the nave had been extended to a point just west of the present screen, the work ceased. It would be two centuries more before the main structure of Henry III's church was complete.

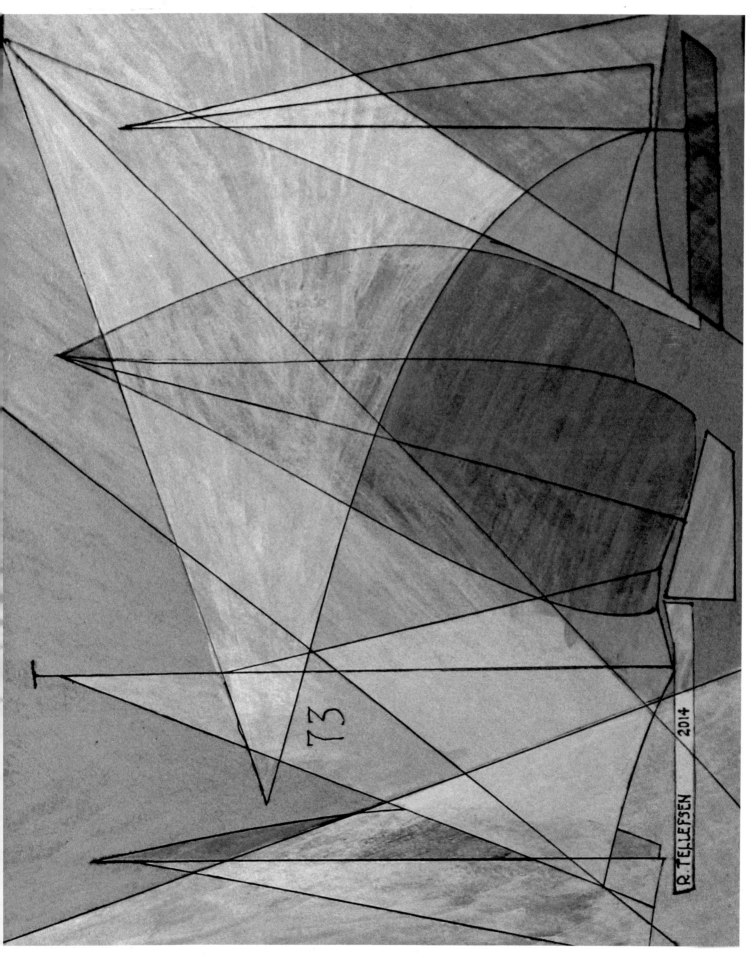

73

R. TELLEFSEN 2014

3 THE CIRCLE OF PLANTAGENETS

WITH HENRY III'S BODY in its tomb raised almost as high as that of his great role model, Edward the Confessor, and within a few feet of it, the precedent was set. It is hard to stand within the circle of Plantagenet kings in the Confessor's Chapel without feeling the enveloping weight of history. The place bears the scars of events and fashions unimaginable when the tombs were set up. The shrine itself, now mainly the work of sixteenth-century restorers, remains the focal point but no longer gleams. The other tombs, varnished by the Victorians in a mistaken attempt to preserve them, have lost most of their colour. Henry III's tomb once glowed with decorated marble almost as brightly as the shrine itself. Its chief splendour remains the magnificent gilt-bronze recumbent effigy of the King, prototype for the Abbey's elite assembly of this form of funerary art.

Though Henry III had urged his heir to finish the Abbey, Edward I's interest waned with the completion in 1291 of his father's tomb and that of his own wife, Eleanor of Castile, who had also been passionately devoted to Edward the Confessor. Eleanor had died in Nottinghamshire late in the previous year, and the grief-stricken King had brought her body home to Westminster, erecting crosses at each resting-place. The last of these was at Charing, just north of the Abbey, from which Charing Cross has its name. Edward arranged a grand funeral for the Queen in the Abbey, and constructed her tomb to the east of his father's, likewise adorned with a gilt-bronze effigy.

Though Edward I's building plans were otherwise focused on castles in Wales rather than the Abbey of Westminster, he still found important uses for the place. He stored his treasure there, and, after he had captured the Stone of Scone from the Scots in 1296, he had it set in a wooden chair and entrusted it to the Abbot's care. Edward's trophy was the roughly hewn block of sandstone on which for generations Scottish kings had been inaugurated. Also known as the Stone of Destiny, it had a potent and mystic significance for the Scots and their monarchy. By carrying it off, Edward meant to ensure that Scotland could never again install

OPPOSITE: The shrine of Edward the Confessor; just beyond is the raised tomb of Henry III, who built the present church to honour his sainted predecessor.

RIGHT: The gilt-bronze tomb effigy of Henry III by the London goldsmith William Torel is an idealised image, not necessarily a true likeness.

ABOVE: Eleanor of Castile, first wife of Edward I. Her gilt-bronze effigy is protected on one side by a fine curved iron grille.

its own king, though in this he was unsuccessful. At the Abbey the new chair, with the Stone in a compartment beneath, was set up in the St Edward's Chapel, next to the shrine's altar. Later it was moved to face the shrine, with its back against the high altar screen. Although properly described as King Edward's Chair, by association it has sometimes been called St Edward's, and is generally known as the Coronation Chair.

On Christmas Eve 1950 the Stone was stolen by a group of young Scottish nationalists in an audacious raid, which has become the stuff of legend, and more recently of film. The point having been made, the Stone was abandoned at Arbroath Abbey (where the Scots had affirmed their independence in 1320) and returned to Westminster. There the story might have ended. In 1996, however, Prime Minister John Major recommended to The Queen that the Stone be returned officially to Scotland. Many were dismayed by this decision, and the ensuing controversy showed that this ancient and talismanic object could still raise passions 700 years after it had been brought to Westminster Abbey. The chair, which had housed it all that time, was moved to a new position in the ambulatory. Even though much damaged by age and abuse, and now empty of its cargo, it still commands attention and awe. It has been used at all coronations from that of Henry IV in 1399, if not before; and since that of James VI, whose accession peacefully united the crowns of Scotland and England, it has been

used at the actual moment of crowning. The Stone is now displayed in Edinburgh Castle. At future coronations it will be returned to its compartment in the Chair, no longer symbolising the English conquest of Scotland but the voluntary and enduring union of the two nations.

Edward's relations with the Abbey nosedived in 1303 when, during his absence on campaign, some of his treasure was stolen from the crypt of the chapter house. The principal culprit was one Richard Pudlicote, who claimed that he had worked alone for three months, chiselling his way in, and concealing his workings by growing hemp. This implausible confession was probably an attempt to shield his accomplices. The walls of the crypt are 5.5 metres (18 feet) thick, so it is more likely that access was gained though a basement window and with assistance. Pudlicote certainly knew the layout of the Abbey and was friendly with several of the monks. A year earlier, he had broken into the refectory and taken some of the Abbey's own plate. The more ambitious burglary of the King's treasure was bungled. Pudlicote panicked as he left, scattering gold, silver and jewels. His associates were unable to dispose of the rest, and all were soon caught. It was assumed that at least some of the monks were implicated, and the whole lot of them were put in the Tower. In the end only Pudlicote and six other laymen were found guilty and executed. Pudlicote was supposedly then flayed. A skin nailed to the door of the Pyx Chamber, next

OPPOSITE: The Coronation Chair, once ornately decorated, was made to house the Stone of Scone, captured by Edward I. The Stone is now kept in Edinburgh Castle, but will be returned to the Abbey for future coronations.

to the chapter house, was later assumed to be his, but has now been identified as cowhide.

There was more mayhem at the Abbey three years later, in 1306, when Edward's son, the Prince of Wales, held an investiture there for new knights. Such was the crowd that two of the knights died and several others fainted. Cavalry horses were sent in to break up the crowd, and the Prince had to conduct proceedings up against, if not actually on, the high altar.

Edward I died the following year and was buried beside his father. Around his tomb is an inscription, thought to have been added in Mary I's reign by Abbot Feckenham: *Edwardus Primus Scotorum Malleus* ('Edward I, Hammer of the Scots') and *Pactum Serva* ('Keep troth'). The tomb never had an effigy. Was this because, as one story goes, he wanted his skeleton to be sent into action against the Scots, dressed in armour and strapped to his horse, as an encouragement to the troops and a terror to the enemy? Was the tomb left with a flat surface to serve as an Easter Sepulchre, where the consecrated Host rested during the annual ceremonies representing Christ's burial and resurrection? Or was it simply that there was no money for one? There was, however, an ornate tester or canopy; this survived the perils of the Reformation and the Civil War, only to be shamefully wrecked by members of the congregation scrambling

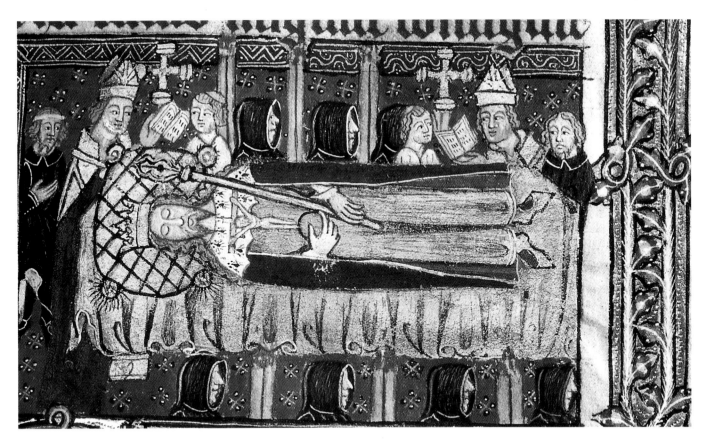

for a vantage point at an eighteenth-century funeral. Not long after this, in 1774, Edward's tomb was opened, and his Purbeck marble coffin was exposed. He was found to be dressed in a tunic of red silk damask, with gold tissue and a mantle of crimson velvet. In his right hand was a sceptre, and in his left a rod surmounted with a dove and oak leaves in white and green enamel. On the head was a gilt crown. The body was 1.9 metres (6 feet 2 inches) in length, so Edward had rightly been called Longshanks.

Edward certainly hammered the Scots, but he did not in fact conquer them. He was more successful in absorbing the Welsh into his kingdom, and by giving the title Prince of Wales to his heir he established a tradition that continues to this day. Edward II did not inherit his father's abilities, and in 1327 he was deposed. Soon afterwards he was murdered at Berkeley Castle, then buried at Gloucester Abbey close by. Westminster saw little of him.

Edward III was just fourteen when he was crowned, though power was retained for a time by his mother Queen Isabelle and her lover Roger Mortimer. A year after his coronation, Edward's new bride Philippa of Hainault came to the Abbey for her crowning. Edward and Philippa were married for forty-two years. On her deathbed Philippa is said to have begged her husband that they might eventually lie buried together, but this was not to be. Though the King spent lavishly on Philippa's tomb, it would remain separate, to the east of his own. In attempting a likeness, if not very successfully, her alabaster effigy, though much damaged, is thought to be the first of its kind.

Edward III's reign was dominated by the first phase of the Hundred Years' War, provoked by Edward's claim to the French throne, and in which the King's eldest son, the Black Prince, won a great reputation. The Prince died the year before his father, so the King was succeeded by his ten-year-old grandson, Richard II. His coronation is said to have been the most splendid yet seen, though it was quite an ordeal for a small boy, and at the end, tired out, he was carried from the Abbey by his tutor, Sir Simon Burley.

Taxation to finance the continuing war in France led ultimately to the Peasants' Revolt (1381), which Richard, still only fourteen, bravely faced down. Before riding out to Smithfield to confront the rebels, he came to the Abbey and prayed at the shrine 'for divine aid where human counsel was altogether wanting'. Though

St Edward had clearly inspired the King that afternoon, he did not always respond positively when appealed to for protection. Not long before the keeper of the Marshalsea Prison had clung to one of the shrine's pillars as escaped prisoners came to get him. They dragged him away and beheaded him outside.

Richard loved the Abbey. He built the great northern entrance, and gave property to support the continuing extension of the nave. His badge of the White Hart was painted on the wall of the Muniment Room, and there are traces of it on the ceiling of the Chapel of Our Lady of the Pew and in the Jerusalem Chamber, part of the Deanery. The full-length portrait of Richard, which now hangs near the west door, is the earliest authentic portrait of an English king.

Richard married Anne of Bohemia in the Abbey in 1382. At her death twelve years later Richard was so heart-broken that he had the manor house at Sheen where she had died burned to the ground. He commissioned a double tomb, which was completed in his lifetime. The effigies were originally hand-in-hand, though the joined hands have long gone. The face of the King is undoubtedly a true likeness. What can Richard have felt when he gazed on it? It was not, however, to be his first resting place. In 1399 he was deposed by his cousin Henry of Bolingbroke, who became King as Henry IV. Soon afterwards Richard was murdered or starved to death at Pontefract Castle, and was buried at King's Langley in Hertfordshire. It was only some years later, on orders from Henry V, that Richard's body was moved to the Abbey and finally placed beside that of his wife.

Henry IV's reign was fraught with trouble, particularly from the barons, the Scots and the Welsh, and his health soon faltered. In 1413 he collapsed as he was praying at the shrine of St Edward. He had been contemplating a pilgrimage to the Holy Land, but he got no further than the Jerusalem Chamber, where the monks took him. His death 'in Jerusalem' had been foretold by soothsayers, so when he momentarily recovered and was told he was 'in Jerusalem' he knew his end had come. He was not, however, buried in the Abbey but in Canterbury Cathedral.

LEFT: Portrait of Henry IV painted posthumously, by an unknown artist. The King's death in the Jerusalem Chamber within the Deanery fulfilled an earlier prophecy.

OPPOSITE: Nothing remains of the medieval quire stalls; their Victorian replacements were gilded and coloured by the Abbey Surveyor in the mid-twentieth century.

According to tradition, Henry IV's eldest son was much affected by his father's death and resolved to abandon his previous wayward lifestyle. In this he was supposedly counselled by one of the Abbey's monks who lived apart as a hermit. If so, this spiritual guidance was highly effective, as Henry V emerged as the epitome of medieval kingship. At his coronation he had been disappointed by the half-finished nave, so he gave further estates to fund its completion. After his great victory over the French at Agincourt on 25 October 1415, a *Te Deum* was sung before the shrine. The further campaigning of England's greatest soldier-king was cut short by dysentery at the age of thirty-three. Henry's disembowelled body was brought back from France to lie in state in St Paul's Cathedral, from where it was brought to the Abbey for a funeral in which three horses were led up the nave

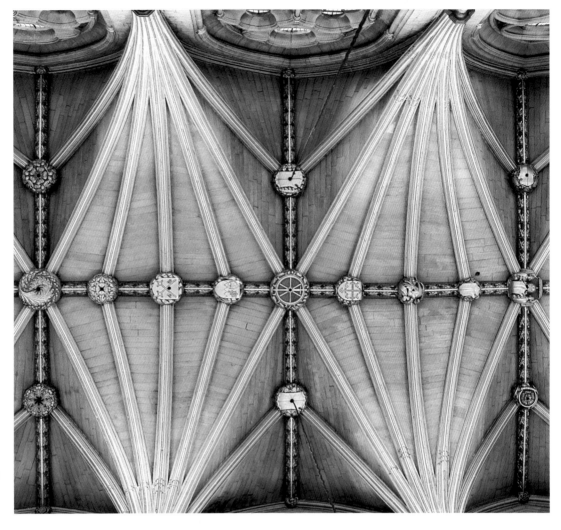

behind the coffin. In 1989 there were echoes of Henry V's achievements at the memorial service for the actor Laurence Olivier, who had so memorably portrayed the King in film, when a recording of his voice was heard speaking the King's words from Shakespeare's play. Henry's oak effigy was originally covered in plates of silver and had a solid silver head. The silver was stolen in 1546. In 1971 a new head was fashioned together with replacement hands modelled on Olivier's.

Henry left instructions for a great chantry chapel to be erected over his tomb. This was a challenge in the confined space east of the shrine; but by building out into the ambulatory and raising spiral stairways above the tombs of Queens Eleanor and Philippa, a distinctive structure was created, where masses were said for the repose of the King's soul. The gathering of royalty immediately round the Confessor was now complete.

4 HENRY VII'S 'WONDER OF THE WORLD'

Henry V's premature death left the throne to his nine-month old son. Crowned in the Abbey when he was eight, Henry VI was clearly a well-behaved child, surveying the scene from his elevated throne 'sadly and wysely'. Two years later, and in consequence of his father's victory, he was crowned King of France in Notre-Dame. Thereafter his reign fell to pieces. Henry grew to be a good and devout man, remembered with affection as founder of Eton College and King's College, Cambridge; but he lacked political judgement. The continuing wars with France sapped his exchequer, and all Henry V's gains were lost. At home he faced increasing opposition from the barons. Then he suffered a mental breakdown, and his right to rule was challenged, leading eventually to civil war between two branches of the Royal Family – the Wars of the Roses. Henry's line came from Edward III's third son, John of Gaunt, the Duke of Lancaster. The rival house of York descended from Edward's fifth son, but also had a descent in the female line from the second son, giving it the better hereditary claim. The Yorkists also had the better of the fight, and their leader seized the throne as Edward IV. Henry was captured and sent to the Tower. In his turn Edward IV alienated many leading figures, and between 1470 and 1471 Henry VI was briefly restored. Edward's heavily pregnant Queen, Elizabeth Woodville, took sanctuary at Westminster Abbey. In the Abbot's house on 2 November (All Souls' Day, when the Church commemorates the dead) she gave birth to the future Edward V, to whom the Abbot and Prior stood godfathers. After Edward IV had recovered the throne he had Henry put back in the Tower and, soon afterwards, murdered.

Henry VI was buried at Chertsey Abbey, with minimum ceremony. Needless to say, this was not what he had planned. Like so many of his predecessors, Henry had been devoted to St Edward and wanted to be buried beside his shrine, even though there was no longer much room. He dismissed a suggestion that his father's tomb could be moved to one side: 'Nay, let hym alone, he lieth lyke a nobyll prince.' Instead he booked his space between the shrine and Henry III's tomb, pacing out the area himself and getting the mason John Thirske to score the outline with an axe. In the 1920s Francis Westlake and Lawrence Tanner, two of the Abbey's leading historians, found the scratches on the mosaic floor when a covering of linoleum was removed.

When Edward IV died suddenly on 4 April 1483 the crown passed to his elder son, aged just twelve; it was not long before the young Edward V's uncle and supposed guardian, Richard, Duke of Gloucester, was plotting to take over. Edward was lodged in the Tower, as was normal before the coronation; but it soon became his prison. Queen Elizabeth again took refuge at Westminster, this time with her younger son Richard, Duke of York, and her five daughters. Gloucester leaned on the Archbishop of Canterbury to persuade Elizabeth to let young Richard join his brother as a playmate. She

ELIZABETH VXOR
EDWARDVS IIII

BELOW: This small wooden statue on a stall in Henry VII's Chapel depicts Henry VI, for whose shrine the chapel was originally conceived.

RIGHT: Elizabeth Woodville, wife of Edward IV, twice took sanctuary in the Abbey; on the first occasion she gave birth to the future Edward V.

immediately regretted her decision, and their parting was tearful. Gloucester then seized the throne as Richard III, having put out a story that Edward IV's children were illegitimate. He had himself crowned with great pageantry on the day for which his nephew's coronation had been set.

When and how the boys died we shall never know. They were last seen, playing together in the Tower, in July. In all probability they were murdered in the following month, on the new King's orders, their bodies quickly buried under a staircase. That is the story told by Sir Thomas More and transmitted by Shakespeare; it remains influential despite the many attempts of Richard III's admirers to acquit him of this and other crimes. It was reinforced in 1674 when skeletons plausibly supposed to be those of the Princes were found beneath stairs in the Tower. Charles II ordered them to be removed to Westminster Abbey, where they now lie in a casket designed by Sir Christopher Wren, set into the wall of the north aisle of Henry VII's Chapel. In 1933 the urn was opened, and the bones were studied by the best techniques then available. The evidence, though not conclusive, suggests they are indeed the remains of the Princes. Modern genetic analysis might settle the matter of their identity, but that is not at the moment in prospect. The Abbey authorities these days take very seriously their responsibilities as custodians of Britain's dead royalty, and would not allow exhumation to satisfy mere curiosity.

Richard III ruled for only two years before his death at the battle of Bosworth, after which his challenger, Henry Tudor, became King as Henry VII. Henry's hered-

ELIZABETHA HENRICI · VXOR VII

itary claim to the throne was shaky. On his father's side he was the grandson of Henry V's widow Catherine of Valois and her second husband Owen Tudor, but he was not a direct descendant of the Lancastrian kings. Through his mother Lady Margaret Beaufort he descended from John of Gaunt, but in a line originally illegitimate and debarred from the succession. Effectively, he was King by conquest. Once in control he astutely married Edward IV's eldest daughter Elizabeth, so uniting the rival houses of York and Lancaster, and ensuring that his heirs would be accepted by the whole nation. This was symbolised by the Tudor rose, blending the white rose emblem of the house of York with a red one retrospectively assigned to Lancaster. Henry nevertheless wanted to demonstrate his Lancastrian credentials by having Henry VI canonised and enshrined

in magnificence at Windsor. This upset the monks of Chertsey (custodians of Henry VI's existing tomb) and those of Westminster (his chosen resting place), both of whom hoped to profit from accommodating the prospective new saint. In the end the honour was awarded to Westminster, and Henry VII began planning a glorious new shrine, which would also form a new and much larger Lady Chapel. The old chapel (and a neighbouring tavern ironically called the White Rose) having been demolished, the foundation stone was laid on 24 January 1503.

What arose on the site has been called one of the architectural wonders of the world. No expense was spared; both the King and his mother poured money into the project. The design, the supreme embodiment of the English Perpendicular style, is attributed to the brothers William and Robert Vertue. Their fan vaulting outshone that of King's College, Cambridge, and St George's Chapel, Windsor, and the rippling curtain walls ensured it was flooded with light. Henry would give his finest image of the Virgin Mary to adorn the tomb, but the chapel's predominant imagery was dynastic. Every surface was peppered with emblems of the Tudor and Beaufort families. Essentially the chapel was an extension of the old royal burial place, expressing the new regime's succession to the Plantagenet kings. Behind the altar was to be the shrine of St Henry VI, with the tomb of Henry VII and his Queen dominating the central space. Tudors yet unborn would gradually surround them, replicating in larger form the arrangement of the Confessor's Chapel.

Although Henry VII's reign was generally peaceful, the underlying tensions remained, and a return to civil war was still feared. Henry therefore sought every means to consolidate his dynasty, and was determined that even in death he would demonstrate his regal authority. His funeral would be on a massive scale, and beyond that was a scheme of ongoing memorial services, for which additional monks were recruited to the Abbey and a community of almsmen and women was founded. Henry's chapel was also home to the lay singing men and boy choristers who were the forbears of the Abbey's modern professional choir. The chapel was virtually an autonomous department within the larger church, a living body continuously praying for dead royalty.

When the old Lady Chapel was pulled down, several tombs were disturbed and their occupants re-located. The remains of eight-year-old Anne Mowbray, Duchess of York, wife of the younger of the Princes in the Tower, were sent to a nunnery in Stepney. Her coffin was unearthed by builders in 1964, causing much public interest. In the following year she was reburied in Henry VII's Lady Chapel, not far from the casket containing the supposed bones of her nine-year-old husband. An odder fate awaited Henry V's Queen, Catherine of Valois, whose coffin remained in the Abbey but was not reburied for almost 300 years. The corpse was occasionally exhibited to tourists; and Samuel Pepys celebrated

his thirty-sixth birthday by kissing the lips, which, if Shakespeare may be believed, once had the beauty to bewitch a king.

Even royalty must compromise with death, and not all of Henry VII's scheme survived him. The pope was said to be demanding so high a price to canonise his uncle that the King decided to wait until the chapel was ready before addressing this additional expense. The building was still unfinished when he died, and his son Henry VIII had other priorities. Though conventionally devout, he had no interest in making the worthy but useless Henry VI a saint. On the contrary, Henry V was his idol, and in time Henry VIII would use the riches of Westminster and every other abbey to pay for his own wars in France. So Henry VI remained at Windsor, to where he had been moved from Chertsey, and the cause for his canonisation lapsed.

Henry VIII did, however, complete the new chapel, and instead of a shrine to Henry VI he commissioned a sumptuous tomb for his parents, the work of the Italian sculptor Pietro Torrigiano. This took six years to complete. Torrigiano went on to design the tomb of Lady Margaret Beaufort, who had died shortly after her grandson's accession. The gilt-bronze effigies of Henry VII, Queen Elizabeth and the Lady Margaret were the last of their kind to be made for the Abbey. Henry VIII might have joined them. In the early years of his reign he planned a tomb for himself and Queen Catherine, also commissioned from Torrigiano. Once it was clear that Henry VI would not be buried at Westminster, Henry VIII decided that his parents' monument should be set behind the altar; he may have meant the central space to be occupied yet more splendidly by himself and his Queen, but before such arrangements could be made Henry had new ideas about his marriage and burial. The next plan was for a tomb at Windsor, using a marble sarcophagus, which he had seized from his fallen minister Cardinal Wolsey. This scheme was also abandoned, so no tomb was ready for occupancy when Henry VIII died in 1547; however, his body was taken to Windsor as he had directed. His son Edward VI ordered the tomb to be completed, though he himself died before this had been done. Curiously the metalwork was all being made in an outbuilding of Westminster Abbey, and the Dean and Chapter were

RIGHT: The vaulting at the east end of Henry VII's Chapel is rich in dynastic emblems, including the Beaufort portcullis and the Tudor rose.

reprimanded by the government when they tried to eject the craftsmen from their premises. During Mary's reign they may have been diverted to the restoration of the Confessor's shrine. By the time Elizabeth came to the throne, her father's golden tomb had become a white elephant, its costs soaring and its religious symbolism no longer acceptable. The half-finished metalwork at Westminster was broken up and sold during the Civil War. The empty sarcophagus was eventually put gloriously to use by enshrining Lord Nelson in St Paul's Cathedral. Henry VIII, however, remained at Windsor. Although Windsor would eventually replace Westminster as the resting place of British royalty, Henry VII's great chapel allowed the tradition of royal burials at Westminster to continue for a further 250 years.

LEFT: One of several gilt-bronze cherubs supporting the royal arms on the tomb of Henry VII and Elizabeth of York.

OPPOSITE: The magnificent Renaissance tomb of Henry VII and his Queen by Pietro Torrigiano erected inside a grille forming a chantry chapel with its own altar, now gone.

5 REFORMATION AND THE TUDORS

Although Henry VIII does not lie within the walls of Westminster Abbey, and visited it only occasionally after his coronation in April 1509, he has had a profound effect on its subsequent history. He made the English Church independent when the papacy would not release him from his marriage to Catherine of Aragon. After eighteen years, this union had produced only a daughter, Mary, and Henry was convinced that chaos would return if he died without a male heir. Though Catherine had been his brother's widow, the marriage to Henry had been allowed by papal dispensation. Pope Clement VII could not be persuaded that his predecessor had exceeded his authority, so in the end Henry took the matter into his own hands. Parliament passed laws severing all connection with Rome and giving the King authority over the Church in England. So as not to appear to be breaking his coronation oath, Henry took the simple expedient of retrospectively rewording it; corrections in the King's

own handwriting now committed him to the protection of the Church only where this was 'nott preiudyciall to hys jurysdyction and dignite r[o]yall'.

With the ecclesiastical machinery now under his control, Henry was in 1533 able to discard Catherine and to marry the woman he now desired, Anne Boleyn. She was then crowned in the Abbey – the last time that a queen consort has had a separate coronation. Yet all this effort seemed in vain when Anne produced only another daughter, Elizabeth. Still desperate for a son, Henry had Anne accused of adultery and beheaded, though not before he had found an excuse to have their marriage annulled as well. He was luckier with Jane Seymour, already selected as his third wife, who at last bore him a son, the future Edward VI; unhappily she died in the process. Although Mary and Elizabeth had been made illegitimate, Henry later restored their rights of succession to the throne. The King's fourth marriage was a political arrangement, and one look at Anne of Cleves

OPPOSITE: Henry VIII, painted by Hans Holbein. Though better remembered as a destroyer of monasteries, he was also a founder of cathedrals including Westminster.

RIGHT: Portrait of a young woman, possibly Catherine of Aragon before her marriage to Henry VIII, painted by Michiel Sittow, c.1503/4. The King later set Catherine aside because she could not produce a male heir to secure the Tudor dynasty.

FAR RIGHT: Portrait of Anne Boleyn by an unknown artist. Anne was Henry VIII's second wife and mother of Elizabeth I. She was also the last queen consort to have a separate coronation.

LEFT: Initial letter 'H' from the charter of 1542, by which Henry VIII returned to the newly established cathedral of Westminster most of the estates he had seized from the old abbey.

was enough to persuade him it was a mistake. It took rather longer to wriggle out of the contract; this lengthy process (including an astonishingly frank disclosure by the King of his sexual capabilities) took place in the refectory of Westminster Abbey during the summer of 1540.

By this time Westminster was actually no longer an abbey. Henry's break with Rome, and his assumption of the title Supreme Head of the Church of England, paved the way for plunder conveniently consistent with a measure of reform. In 1536 shrines, relics and images of saints were destroyed, and even Westminster Abbey was stripped of much of its finery. The golden feretory that housed St Edward's coffin was removed and melted down. Other parts of the shrine were simply strewn around. Fearful for the very bones of their Saint, the monks hid the body. Then between 1536 and 1540 all monasteries were dissolved, and their assets were seized by the Crown. Westminster was almost the last survivor when, on 16 January 1540, the monks gathered in the chapter house to sign the deed of surrender.

Some part of what Henry took with one hand he gave back with the other. While many monasteries would be left to become picturesque ruins, Westminster was given new life as the cathedral of a new diocese. Though Henry had already invested in its future by commissioning his own tomb, he was probably more concerned to preserve the place of coronation. The foundation may have been transformed, but most of those employed there simply changed their colours. Abbot William Boston reverted to his family name and became Dean as William Benson, with five other ex-monks among the twelve canons. Together they constituted the governing body ('The Dean and Chapter'). The new establishment also included twelve minor canons, a gospeller and epistoler, twelve lay singing men, ten boy choristers and their master, two sextons, other officials and twelve 'poor men decayed in the King's service' – the almsmen. The monastic school was put on a more solid footing, to comprise two masters and forty scholars, and a new schoolroom was built for them. The Dean and Chapter also had to support twenty students and ten readers at the universities of Oxford and Cambridge, the latter being the original regius professors. To pay for all this the King returned to the cathedral many of the estates that had once belonged to the monastery, most of them given by his predecessors and other members of the Royal Family.

When Henry VIII died in 1547 his son and successor, Edward VI, was just nine. His coronation was abridged, notionally in deference to his age, but mainly to curtail the Catholic rites still in force. Instead of a sermon Archbishop Cranmer delivered a brief defence of such ceremonial as had remained. Those who ruled in the boy-King's name moved swiftly to introduce Protestant ideas

OPPOSITE: Portrait of Edward VI by an unknown artist, c.1547. During his short reign Protestantism was firmly established; English services were introduced, and churches were stripped of their ornaments and treasures.

and practices. The first Book of Common Prayer (1549) put all services into English, and the second version (1552) made more radical changes to their structure. Some of the new liturgies and their music were tested out in the Abbey. At the same time the spoliation continued, as Catholic furnishings were seized or sold. In May 1553 the King's agents carried away virtually everything that remained, leaving just a few pieces of plate, some cloths and a little drape for the Dean's stall.

Two months later Edward died, still only sixteen. He and his Council had schemed to by-pass his Catholic half-sister Mary (and Elizabeth as well) and to place his Protestant cousin Lady Jane Grey on the throne. The coup failed, and Mary was warmly welcomed in London. She allowed Edward a Protestant funeral in the Abbey, but his only memorial is a small stone given in 1966 by Christ's Hospital, one of the many schools he founded. Mary had immediately restored the Mass and other Catholic services, and at her coronation on 1 October 1553 all the old ceremonies were observed. Because no holy oil had been consecrated in England for several years, a new supply had to be sent from abroad. It used to be said that Mary thought the ancient Coronation Chair had been desecrated when Edward sat in it, and so had a replacement made for herself. This wholly imaginary story was coloured by association with a chair surviving at Winchester Cathedral, which Mary almost certainly did use at her marriage there to the future Philip II of Spain. There were moves to have Philip crowned King of England; this never happened, but he was given the unique status of King Consort. He came once with the Queen to Westminster Abbey, attending High Mass before the State Opening of Parliament in 1554.

By this time the Abbey had been purged of its Protestant clergy. Dean Richard Cox was immediately arrested, though he escaped and fled abroad. Soon afterwards most of the canons were deprived of their livings for having married (clerical marriage, legalised under Edward but prohibited again under Mary, was an obvious indication of Protestant sympathies). This enabled Mary to pack the Abbey with men of her own choosing. The new Dean was Hugh Weston, who took a leading part in prosecuting Archbishop Cranmer for heresy. The

The Burning of William Flower in St Margaret's Church-yard, Westminster.

canons included a Spanish priest who had served Catherine of Aragon; with him lodged one of King Philip's confessors. Though Westminster thus became a high-profile Catholic community, Mary had bolder plans. Parliament had agreed to restore Catholic services and allegiance to Rome, but it would not make people return lands or goods that had belonged to the monasteries. If monks were wanted, new monasteries would have to be founded. Mary and her spiritual mentor, Cardinal Pole, took the lead by bringing the Benedictines back to Westminster. This involved dissolving the cathedral foundation and ejecting the secular clergy. Dean Weston and his colleagues were unhappy, but were compensated with other posts. The new monastery was inaugurated in November 1556; two monks were survivors from old Westminster Abbey, and most of the rest had been in other Benedictine houses. Their Abbot was John Feckenham, latterly Dean of St Paul's. His great achievement was to complete the restoration of the Confessor's shrine, patched together from what remained of the old structure and topped with a new wooden feretory in the classical style.

Anne of Cleves, who had lived on quietly in England since Henry rejected her, welcomed the return of Catholicism and attended Mary's coronation. When she died in August 1557 she was buried in the Abbey. Mary herself died on 17 November 1558, a sad and isolated figure. Like her father she had been desperate for a direct heir to sustain her work. Dean Weston had published a prayer when it was thought she was pregnant, but all that grew inside her was an ovarian cancer. Philip returned to Spain, and Mary's popularity disintegrated as she began to enforce Catholicism through terror. Over 300 Protestants were executed by burning, chief among them Archbishop Cranmer, and Bishop Nicholas Ridley, who had been a Canon of Westminster. As a result Mary's death was greeted with rejoicing and relief. Since Cardinal Pole had died the same day, it seemed that God was rescuing the Protestant cause. Elizabeth was expected to guide the nation back in that direction; so she did, but, unlike Mary, she waited till Parliament met before altering the status quo. Mary was buried in the north aisle of Henry VII's Chapel, attended by the monks she had restored; in her will she made a final benefaction to them. It was still within a context of a Catholic mass that Elizabeth was crowned on 15 January 1559, though there were significant changes: the Epistle and Gospel were read in English as well as Latin, and the consecrated host was not elevated for veneration. With no new archbishop yet chosen for Canterbury, and all the senior bishops appointed by Mary refusing to officiate, it was the lowly Bishop of Carlisle who eventually did the honours.

Ten days later Elizabeth was back at the Abbey for the mass before the State Opening of Parliament, and gave an immediate signal of her intentions. When Feckenham and his monks met her with ceremonial torches, she told them that she could see well enough. The parliament that then began defined the enduring shape of the Church of England, and also sealed the fate of the restored monastery. A new act of dissolution handed Westminster and the few other Marian refoundations back to the Crown, and the monks left for the final time at Midsummer. Though it might seem to have been a dead end, this short episode in Westminster Abbey's history was vital. The old monastery had no ecclesiastical overlord save the pope. Henry VIII's cathedral had necessarily slotted into the normal system, first under its own Bishop and then the Bishop of London.

VIVat, VInCat, Regnet,
ELISABETHA,
ngLIæ FranCIæ, aC Hiberniæ
ReGIna,
FIDeI DefenfatrIX
HenrICI 8.ᵛⁱ RegIs F;
nno regnI sVI.XXXVII

RIGHT: Westminster School has a particular affection for Elizabeth I. Queen's Scholars gather round a bust of her, which was commissioned in 2003 to mark the fiftieth anniversary of the coronation of Elizabeth II.

With Mary the church of Westminster regained its autonomy and this was retained when Elizabeth made her own foundation, the present collegiate church.

This was established by letters patent of 21 May 1560, which also appointed the new Dean, William Bill, and twelve canons. In most respects it was a return to the arrangements made by Henry VIII twenty years before; the important difference was that Elizabeth's foundation belonged to no diocese, becoming what is known as a Royal Peculiar. (A 'peculiar' is any church not subject to the bishop whose diocese otherwise covers the area.) The deans and canons are still appointed directly by the Crown, and enjoy a certain independence from the rest of the Church of England. This allows them, as one recent dean put it, to be 'irresponsibly responsible'; and although the position has never been tested very far, it has meant the Dean and Chapter have some freedom in the direction and expression of their ministry. Furthermore Elizabeth I never followed up her foundation with statutes; these were drafted, but have served simply as guidelines, refined as circumstances change.

Elizabeth's foundation also marks an important stage in the development of Westminster School.

Henry VIII's establishment had in fact kept going during the monastic restoration; it now became again part of a larger collegiate body. Eventually the School would become a separate institution, though still linked to the Abbey through shared buildings and in many other ways. Elizabeth I took a keen interest in the School, and several times attended one of the Latin plays for which the Westminster boys became famous. Every year the School holds its commemoration service on her accession day, 17 November, and lays flowers on her tomb.

That anniversary was long celebrated as a national holiday, recalling with joy and relief the death of a Catholic Queen and the triumph of her Protestant successor. In 2008, to mark the 450th anniversary of those events in a more ecumenical spirit, the Abbey held a Festival of Commemoration in which Mary and Elizabeth were equally remembered. At an evensong attended by representatives of the Archbishop of Canterbury and the Cardinal Archbishop of Westminster, the tomb in which both Queens lie was censed, and the Dean of Westminster prayed for all those of different convictions 'who laid down their lives for Christ and conscience sake in the time of … Mary and Elizabeth'.

MEMORIAE AETERNAE.
ELIZABETHAE ANGLIAE, FRANCIAE, ET HIBERNIAE
REGINAE, R HENRICI VIII FILIAE, R HEN VII NEPTI, R
ED IIII PRONEPTI, PATRIAE PARENTI RELIGIONIS
ET BONARVM ARTIVM ALTRICI, PLVRIMARVM
LINGVARVM PERITIA, PRAECLARIS TVM ANIMI
TVM CORPORIS DOTIBVS, REGIISQ VIRTVTIBVS
SVPRA SEXVM PRINCIPI
INCOMPARABILI
IACOBVS MAGNAE BRITANNIAE, FRANCIAE, ET
HIBERNIAE REX, VIRTVTVM ET REGNORVM
HAERES, BENE MERENTI PIE
POSVIT

6

CIVIL WAR
AND THE STUARTS

Elizabeth died at Richmond on 24 March 1603. There was much public grief as the great funeral procession wound its way to Westminster, where she was buried in the same vault as her grandparents. On the other hand the old Queen had outlived most of her contemporaries and even, many felt, her usefulness. Great things were expected of her successor, James VI of Scotland, whose peaceful accession to the English throne forged the link centuries of warfare had failed to achieve. As yet it was only a personal union of two crowns, but people now began to speak of Great Britain. James had already been crowned in Scotland. When he came to the Abbey to receive the English crown he sat in Edward I's chair above the Scottish coronation stone.

One grievance from the past may have been resolved, but another remained. James was the son and successor of Mary Queen of Scots, whose tumultuous and tragic life had been ended by Elizabeth. After Mary had been forced to abdicate she had sought asylum in England, only to find herself immediately imprisoned. Mary was Elizabeth's nearest cousin and heir; she was also a

Catholic and the focus of many plots against the Queen's life. She foolishly became involved in one such plot, and Elizabeth with great reluctance ordered her execution. Mary was beheaded at Fotheringhay Castle, Northamptonshire, on 8 February 1587. Only after much agonising over protocol for which there was no precedent was she buried in nearby Peterborough Cathedral. James, who had succeeded to her throne as an infant and had been brought up a Protestant, coped well with an impossible position, expressing outrage but doing nothing to jeopardise his own prospective English inheritance.

Once on the English throne, James determined to give his mother a finer tomb in Westminster Abbey; since the issues were still highly sensitive, James recognised that he must balance his act of filial piety by simultaneously honouring his English predecessor. So he commissioned two monuments. The grander one, for his mother, which would stand in the south aisle of Henry VII's Chapel, was made by Cornelius Cure, one of the country's leading sculptors. The lesser-known Maximilian Colt was entrusted with the smaller monument to Elizabeth in the north aisle, to which her body

OPPOSITE: Elizabeth I's monument by Maximilian Colt. Within the tomb the Queen's coffin rests directly above that of her half-sister Mary I. The railings are modern reconstructions.

RIGHT: Mary Queen of Scots was executed in 1587 by order of her cousin Elizabeth I. Mary's body only came to the Abbey after her son had succeeded to Elizabeth's throne as James I in 1603.

was to be moved from her grandparents' vault. This plan rather backfired, since Elizabeth's tomb was completed first, in 1606, and was much admired. Cure died still at work on Mary's tomb, which was left for his dilatory son to complete in 1613, somewhat reduced from its original design. But Mary's effigy is still set higher than Elizabeth's, and under a more sumptuous canopy. She is the only ruler of a foreign country to lie in Westminster Abbey, and her tomb is the only monument there to any Stuart monarch. It is indeed the only contemporary tomb effigy of any Scottish ruler, all those of her predecessors having been destroyed at the Reformation. The other Stuarts buried in the Abbey are in the south aisle of Henry VII's Chapel, having only a simple inscription above their graves.

Elizabeth's tomb also contains the remains of her sister Mary. For a time Elizabeth had thought of finishing her father's tomb and of raising one to her brother, but had no plans for her sister. Nothing marked Mary I's grave save stones taken from altars destroyed at the Reformation. It was left to James I to tidy up the Tudor dead. What regard he had for Elizabeth was diluted by her being his mother's killer, and by the increasing frequency with which his English subjects recalled the glories of her reign. Like any Protestant he was appalled by the memory of Mary's regime. Yet for a moment in the 1600s there was some hope that the Reformation rift might be mended, and James saw himself as a bridge-builder. He

set on the tomb of the Tudor Queens words that seem to anticipate the ecumenism of our own time: 'Partners in throne and grave, here we sleep, Elizabeth and Mary, sisters in hope of the resurrection'. These sentiments provided the focus for the Abbey's commemoration of both Queens in 2008. It is nevertheless only Elizabeth's effigy that rests above the tomb. Most of the work is original, though the railings are later, while the gilded collar and the crown are modern replacements for stolen originals.

Elizabeth I's tomb effigy was the last of its kind in the Abbey, ending the sequence begun with Henry III. After Elizabeth, the Abbey's royal burials are marked only by inscriptions on coffins and paving stones. In some cases their location was forgotten, and only detective work by the great Victorian Dean A.P. Stanley rediscovered the tomb of James I in the vault containing the bodies of Henry VII and Elizabeth of York. Not until the twentieth century was another tomb effigy made for a British monarch – that of Queen Victoria in the Mausoleum at Frogmore. However, the Abbey Museum is home to another famous set of life-size royal effigies, which extend from the fourteenth century to the eighteenth. It was long customary at royal funerals to place a clothed mannequin of the deceased above the coffin. Several of these models were kept in the Abbey and became tourist attractions. Although popularly called waxworks, the early ones are made of wood and plaster. The oldest to

BELOW: Charles II's wax effigy, dressed in his own Garter robes, was not actually carried at his funeral but was placed over the vault where he was buried.

survive is that of Edward III, the body intact though the clothes are long gone. The heads have been the most enduring components, and those of the consorts of Richard II, Henry V, Edward IV and James I can still be seen. Mary I's head, still with much of its original paint, is particularly striking. The figure of Elizabeth I is an eighteenth-century replacement, though wearing some clothes from the decayed original. It is the lively full figure of Charles II in Garter robes that steals the show. By comparison William III, Mary II and Queen Anne look like the waxworks they actually are.

The Stuart dynasty has otherwise left little visible mark on the Abbey. James I planned a grandiose tomb for his elder son, Prince Henry, whose premature death in 1612 disappointed the expectations of many. This was never built. Only Henry's little sisters Sophia (aged three) and Mary (aged two) represent the family among the Abbey's great collection of funerary sculpture. James was succeeded by his younger son, Charles I, who was much concerned to restore to the Church of England some of the dignified furnishings and ceremonial that had been swept aside at the Reformation. In this he was supported by Archbishop William Laud, who had been a Canon of Westminster. The King's religious policy was one of the main causes of the Civil War, which broke out in 1642. The King's opponents thought that the Reformation had not gone nearly far enough, and when their opportunity came they introduced much more radical changes. After the King's military defeat he was put on trial in Westminster Hall, and was adjudged to have committed treason by making war on his own people. On 30 January 1649 he was beheaded outside Whitehall Palace, within sight of the Abbey. Burial with Anglican rites was allowed him, but at Windsor rather than Westminster to prevent a large gathering. The monarchy in England was abolished and so too was the hierarchy of the Anglican Church. The Dean and Chapter had fled from the Abbey at the start of the war, and in their place the republican government appointed preachers of its own choosing. Only Westminster School stayed much as before, though now governed by a committee responsible to Parliament.

Oliver Cromwell, the country squire whose generalship had won the Civil War, became head of state. He refused the title of King, but for his inauguration as Lord Protector in Westminster Hall in 1657, the Coronation Chair was brought over from the Abbey. On Cromwell's death the following year he was given a kingly funeral in the Abbey, complete with an effigy on which was placed the crown he had declined in life. The opponents of monarchy could not, it seems, quite do without it. Even the hereditary principle was reintroduced when Cromwell's son, Richard, who had none of his father's ability, succeeded him. Opinion moved rapidly in favour of restoring the real dynasty, and Charles II was recalled, entering London on 29 May 1660. Early in the following year, just before the anniversary of Charles I's execution, the bodies of Cromwell and other republican leaders were taken from the Abbey, hanged for public execration and unceremoniously buried. With the monarchy were restored the Anglican Church and its liturgy, and West-minster Abbey was returned to its proper authorities. Because most of the ancient regalia had been destroyed by the republicans, new pieces were made for Charles II's coronation on 23 April 1661.

Though Charles II was received into the Roman Church on his deathbed, he was buried in the Abbey as an Anglican. His brother and heir, James II, had taken the path to Rome much earlier, and considerable efforts had been made to exclude him from the throne as a result. At first the nation accepted the Catholic King, reassured by the expectation that he would soon be succeeded by his Protestant elder daughter Mary. When James fathered a son who was certain to be brought up a Catholic, his opponents orchestrated the Bloodless Revolution of 1688. James was driven into exile, and in his place Mary and her husband William of Orange, ruler of the Netherlands, became joint-monarchs. After James died in Paris in 1701 he was never properly buried, in the forlorn hope that his body would be taken to Westminster Abbey when his dynasty was restored. The coffin disappeared during the French Revolution.

Mary II died at the end of 1694, and was buried in the Abbey early in the following year. She has her memorial in the magnificently sombre music that the Abbey's organist Henry Purcell composed for the occasion.

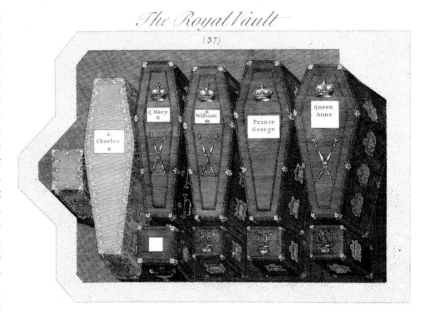

William III reigned alone till his death in 1702, when he was succeeded by James II's younger daughter Anne.

While the Stuarts make little impression above ground at Westminster Abbey, they lie in profusion beneath it. Theirs was a dynasty touched by many misfortunes, including high infant mortality. Before he became a Catholic, the future James II had four sons. All died in early childhood, and each of the four little coffins in the Abbey vault now represents a history of England that did not happen. The boys would surely have been brought up as Protestants like their sisters, and had any one of them grown to adulthood, the birth of another son to James II in 1688 would not have prompted a revolution. Queen Anne and her husband, Prince George of Denmark, had five living children and seven more stillborn; nine of them are buried in the Abbey, including the eldest, William, Duke of Gloucester. His death in 1700, just after his eleventh birthday, likewise changed the world. It became essential to secure the Protestant succession, and the Act of Settlement passed the following year required every future monarch to belong to the Church of England. Thus James II's heirs and other Catholic lines were by-passed, and Anne was followed in

ABOVE: Coffins in the Stuart vault: Charles II, Mary II and her husband William III, Queen Anne and her husband Prince George of Denmark.

OPPOSITE: James II, as Duke of York, who succeeded his brother Charles II only to lose the throne three years later. A portrait by Sir Peter Lely.

DVKE OF YORK

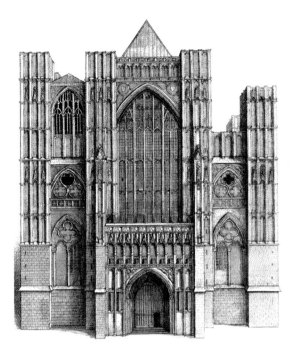

1714 by her distant Protestant cousin, the Elector George Louis of Hanover. Under the German dynasty the power of the monarchy declined, while Britain developed as a democracy and an imperial power.

George I had already locked up his wife because of her alleged infidelity, so he was crowned alone. He was buried back in Hanover, where he had died. His successor George II had a closer relationship with his English subjects, and a very much better one with his wife. That is not to say he was faithful to her, but he was tolerably fond of her. When Queen Caroline died in 1737, the King commissioned a pair of coffins with detachable sides so that they could eventually lie side by side. By the time George II was buried beside Caroline in 1760 he had lived longer than any previous English king. He was the last to be buried in the Abbey, ending the tradition of almost 700 years. Some further royal burials took place there during the remainder of the eighteenth century, including that of George II's third son, William Augustus, Duke of Cumberland (died 1765), whose victory over the Jacobite army at Culloden in 1746 extinguished all hope of a Stuart restoration. Another Duke of Cumberland (Henry Frederick, brother of George III, died 1790) was the last member of the Royal Family to be buried in the Abbey. Instead, increasing use was made of St George's Chapel, Windsor, and George III was himself buried there in 1820. All subsequent royal burials have been in St George's or the nearby mausoleum at Frogmore.

While the Hanoverian era closed one strand of the Abbey's royal story, it began another. By this time party politics had developed, and new ways of buying and rewarding political support were needed. Hitherto there was nothing between a plain knighthood and the exclusive Orders of the Garter and the Thistle. So in 1725 the Prime Minister, Sir Robert Walpole, enthusiastically assisted by Garter King of Arms, John Anstis, devised the larger but still prestigious Order of the Bath. The name was taken from an older form of knighthood, which had been given as a special honour, usually before coronations. The knights had taken a ritual bath to symbolise purification before their investiture; this ritual had last been observed at the coronation of Charles II in 1661. The knights did not form an Order in the modern sense because they never assembled together again and retained no insignia. Nevertheless here was a venerable tradition on which the new Order could be built. Where the Garter knights had St George's, Windsor, for their spiritual home, the Bath knights would have Henry VII's Chapel in Westminster Abbey. As at Windsor, the knights' banners, swords and helmets would be placed over their stalls. The Dean of Westminster became Dean of the Order, wearing a crimson mantle like the knights and playing an important part in their installation service. A magnificent painting by Canaletto, now in the Deanery, shows the 1749 Bath procession in all its crimson finery emerging from the Abbey, itself recently capped with its distinctive western towers. In fact the Bath procession is incidental to the painting, the main purpose of which was to show the newly added western towers. Since the finishing of the nave 300 years earlier the west front had presented a lop-sided appearance. Twin towers had been planned, but the Reformation had put an end to all such schemes. It was eventually the design of Sir Christopher Wren, the Abbey's Surveyor, completed by his pupil Nicholas Hawkesmoor in 1749, that gave the Abbey its distinctive face.

7 CROWNING GLORIES

OF ALL THE CEREMONIAL seen in the Abbey, the coronation has pride of place. It is the fullest manifestation of royal splendour, and the expression of a people's political identity. This has been so since primitive times, even when the event was used to legitimise an accession achieved through intrigue and bloodshed. The ceremony has been retained in Britain while all other European monarchies have abandoned it, though some still display regalia at simpler inaugurations. Even the coronation of the popes has ceased, the last being that of Paul VI in 1963. Following the death of her mother in 2002, The Queen was left as the only crowned head in Europe. Because only Britain sustains the tradition, the fascination with Westminster Abbey as the coronation church has become ever greater.

Thirty-nine monarchs have been crowned in Westminster Abbey since the Norman conquest, thirty-one of them in the present church, and in thirty-eight ceremonies (because William III and Mary II were crowned together as joint-monarchs). There have also been fifteen separate coronations of consorts, the last being Anne Boleyn in 1533. Henry VIII's next wife, Jane Seymour, did not live long enough to enjoy the coronation being arranged for her, and no plans were made to crown wives four, five and six. Philip of Spain missed out because it was feared he might claim to rule in his own right after Mary I's death. Charles I's Catholic wife refused to be crowned with her husband, or even to watch the ceremony from the screened enclosure prepared for her. Charles II's bride was another Catholic and was not crowned. Since then no occasion for separate coronation has arisen, though this might yet happen. It can more confidently be predicted that Westminster Abbey will never again see the coronation of an heir in his father's lifetime, as Henry II arranged for his son Henry in 1170. This attempt to write history in advance misfired badly, since the Young King, as he was called, rebelled against his father and died before succeeding him.

The coronation rite has been altered on almost every occasion to suit new conditions or demands. This has usually meant the accommodation of immediate political realities. Latterly, the reshaping has been informed by scholarship, restoring what had been lost and cutting away superfluous accretions. However, the essential framework has remained intact through the centuries, and in this the architecture of Westminster Abbey has itself been a key factor. Not for nothing is its central space, when prepared for a coronation, called the stage or theatre. In most great churches the choir stalls cut into this area. At Westminster Abbey they are west of it, truncating the nave but opening up the transepts to create a theatre-in-the-round for the greatest show in the world. Yet it is not all played to the galleries; there are intimate and holy moments, which the structure of the sacrarium hides from general view.

The coronation takes place within the context of the Eucharist. At the start is the Recognition, when the sovereign is presented at the four corners of the stage, and the people shout their acclamation; in medieval times it was essential that the new ruler should be seen and

OPPOSITE: The coronation of a king and queen, from the fourteenth-century manuscript called the *Liber Regalis*, the definitive text of the English coronation service.

RIGHT: The coronation of a queen as illustrated in the Litlyngton Missal.

acknowledged. Then comes the swearing of an oath, the fundamental contract between ruler and ruled, echoing the promise made in 973 by King Edgar that he would maintain peace, administer justice, and exercise equity and mercy. Having established identity and good faith, the monarch is then anointed with oil. This is the most sacred part of the service, a solemn act of dedication modelled on religious ordination. There follows the investiture with robes (again closely resembling priestly vestments) and regalia, culminating in the actual crowning. Anointing and investiture take place immediately in front of the altar. The monarch, arrayed with all the symbols of majesty, is then escorted to a throne set high at the very centre of the stage, where dignitaries kneel in acts of homage.

Much of the Order of Service still used derives from two beautifully illuminated manuscripts preserved in the Abbey's library: the *Liber Regalis* made for the coronation of Richard II in 1377, and a missal commissioned by Abbot Nicholas Litlyngton in 1383. In Catholic times the ceremonial was set within a votive mass of the Holy Ghost. Since 1603 the Communion Service of the Book of Common Prayer has been followed. The Communion was omitted in 1685 in deference to the Catholic King James II, who then agreed to go through with the rest of the Protestant ritual. This even-handedness succeeded only to the extent of upsetting both sides in equal measure. The French ambassador reported that the King and Queen, still regarding the Abbey ceremony as bogus, had themselves secretly crowned by Catholic rites the day before. On the way to the Abbey the canopy carried by four Barons of the Cinque Ports (one being Pepys) collapsed on James's head, and during the service the ill-fitting crown almost fell from it. Such mishaps were invariably read as omens, though the stories attach with suspicious consistency to kings who came to grief. James II himself was driven from the throne after three years. Edward II gave offence by rushing through the solemnities and allowing a prominent role to his close friend Piers Gaveston. Edward was deposed, then murdered in a peculiarly painful way. The ten-year-old Richard II did nothing worse at his coronation than fall asleep and lose a slipper; but he too was deposed and murdered. At Charles I's coronation the

ABOVE: James II processing from Westminster Hall to the Abbey for his coronation in 1685. The canopy-bearer in the centre foreground is Samuel Pepys.

LEFT: This engraving of Charles II's coronation in 1661 is the first realistic image of the ceremony within the Abbey.

people had to be prompted to cheer, and then there was an earthquake. Charles was publicly executed.

Although the texts of the coronation liturgy survive from the Middle Ages, and reports of the ceremonial become increasingly more detailed, visual evidence is weak until the end of the seventeenth century. Medieval coronation scenes are icons, not realistic depictions. The first authentic images show the outdoor processions at the coronations of Edward VI and Elizabeth I. From the latter there are also some sketch plans of the stage inside the Abbey. Not until the coronation of Charles II in 1661 is there a decent interior view. For the next coronation, that of James II in 1685, a series of panoramic prints was published at the King's command by Francis Sandford, one of the heralds. This work was hugely influential, serving as a model for future coronations, and helping scholars to draw infer-

ences about previous coronations. Incidentally, it also gives much information about the ordinary appearance of the Abbey at the time.

Sandford's prints show how extensive the temporary galleries had already become. This tendency increased during the eighteenth century, as the religious aspect of the coronation was subordinated to public spectacle. Galleries were even built above the high altar. Tickets were sold, stalls were set up in the Abbey to sell food and drink, while the more thrifty brought their own. The diarist William Hickey noted that at the coronation of George III in 1761 the congregation, unable to hear a word of the sermon, took the opportunity to start their picnics, so that the 'general clattering of knives, forks and plates' then prompted a 'universal burst of laughter'. It must be admitted that all state ceremonies of the period were characterised by muddle and irreverence, if not outright disorder.

George IV waited for the throne longer than any previous heir, and when he eventually succeeded to it, in 1820, he was determined that his coronation should be the most lavish ever seen. The national mood was buoyant after the defeat of Napoleon, and Parliament voted an unprecedented £250,000 to indulge the King's notions of pageantry, which were heavily influenced by the antiquarian imaginings of Sir Walter Scott. The scene in the Abbey was, as Scott himself wrote, 'beyond measure magnificent ... filled to overcrowding with all that Britain has of beautiful and distinguished'. The party was a little spoiled by the arrival of Queen Caroline, whom the King had been trying hard to divorce, but who had determined to seek her own coronation, with the King or without. She cannot seriously have supposed that this would be available on demand in the Abbey, and by turning up uninvited she doubtless merely hoped to make a scene. This she certainly did, but was met by several hefty stewards (in fact boxers hired by the King for this purpose) who slammed the door in her face.

George IV was therefore crowned alone, weighed down by the finery he had designed for himself, which included a long curly wig. One of those unimpressed by the spectacle was Harriet Arbuthnot, wife of a politician, who wrote of her King that 'anyone who could have seen his disgusting figure ... would have been quite sick'. Lady Palmerston was shocked by a 'mixing up the Sacrament and the Greatest Ceremonies of the Church with all Vanity and Jokes'.

There was an understandable reaction against all this extravagance when George's brother succeeded him as William IV in 1830. The new King, at sixty-four the old-est ever to ascend the throne, would have happily done without a coronation, which he regarded as superstitious flummery. The public mood had changed, and radical agitation was challenging all the traditional institutions. There was also a warning from abroad: Charles X of France had set the tone for his autocratic regime with an even more flamboyant coronation than George IV's, and had just been ousted in favour of a simpler style of monarchy. William eventually agreed to a coronation, but on a much reduced scale. The banquet in Westminster Hall and many attendant ceremonies were dropped, and other economies kept the budget to £30,000, little more than a tenth of what George IV had spent. There was still a good deal of unedifying behaviour; as was customary, medals were simply tossed to the congregation, so that even the judges had to scramble about 'like so many rams in a pen' to collect their souvenirs. Again the elderly King cut a poor figure. Nonetheless, the vital thing was that the tradition had been kept alive.

Decorum began to return with the coronation of the young Queen Victoria in 1838, though this could have gone too far. *The Times* thought that the anointing was 'more recommended by antiquity than delicacy' and would probably be omitted. In fact the Queen was anointed, but not on the breast, and at the homage she was kissed by the kneeling peers on the hand rather than the cheek. For the first time we have the monarch's own account of the proceedings. The Queen noted in her diary that the Archbishop put the ring on the wrong finger, and she had only managed to take it off 'at last with great pain'. She feigned horror at finding the

Confessor's Chapel turned into a buffet, with 'what was called an altar covered with sandwiches, bottles of wine, etc.', though perhaps in reality she was a little amused.

In 1887 Victoria celebrated her Golden Jubilee with a service in the Abbey. There was no precedent for this, and some expected the Queen to appear with full robes and regalia. Victoria, already a widow for a quarter of a century, never discarded her mourning, but for this festivity she added the Garter insignia and a miniature crown. She sat in the Coronation Chair, which had been given a heavy coat of dark varnish, subsequently removed with much painstaking effort.

Edward VII's coronation in 1902 was dramatically postponed at the last minute. As the final rehearsal was taking place in the Abbey, it was announced that the King had appendicitis, and would undergo surgery in a few hours. Immediately an impromptu service of intercession was held. The King recovered well, and when the coronation went ahead two months later he was more concerned for the health of Archbishop Benson, who was elderly and almost blind. Despite having his lines on large-print prompt scrolls, he kept making

little mistakes. He also put the crown on back to front, and in trying to correct matters he almost dropped it. Despite the problems, Edward VII's coronation set the standard for the twentieth century.

Two developments were of special relevance to the Westminster community. By tradition the monarch presents a quantity of fine fabric to the Abbey. This offering had dwindled to a symbolic fragment, but Edward VII and Queen Alexandra gave a large quantity of red velvet, which was made into vestments and a covering for the shrine. George V and Queen Mary gave the altar hangings used at their coronation and those that followed. The offerings in 1937 and 1952 were again made into vestments for the Abbey clergy. By custom the scholars of Westminster School are the first to acclaim monarch and consort as they enter the Abbey, but their cries of *Vivat Rex* and *Vivat Regina* had become random and undignified. For Edward VII's coronation, the composer Sir Hubert Parry worked them into his sumptuous new setting of the processional psalm, *I was glad*.

George V's coronation came just nine years after his father's, so many of the participants had a measure of

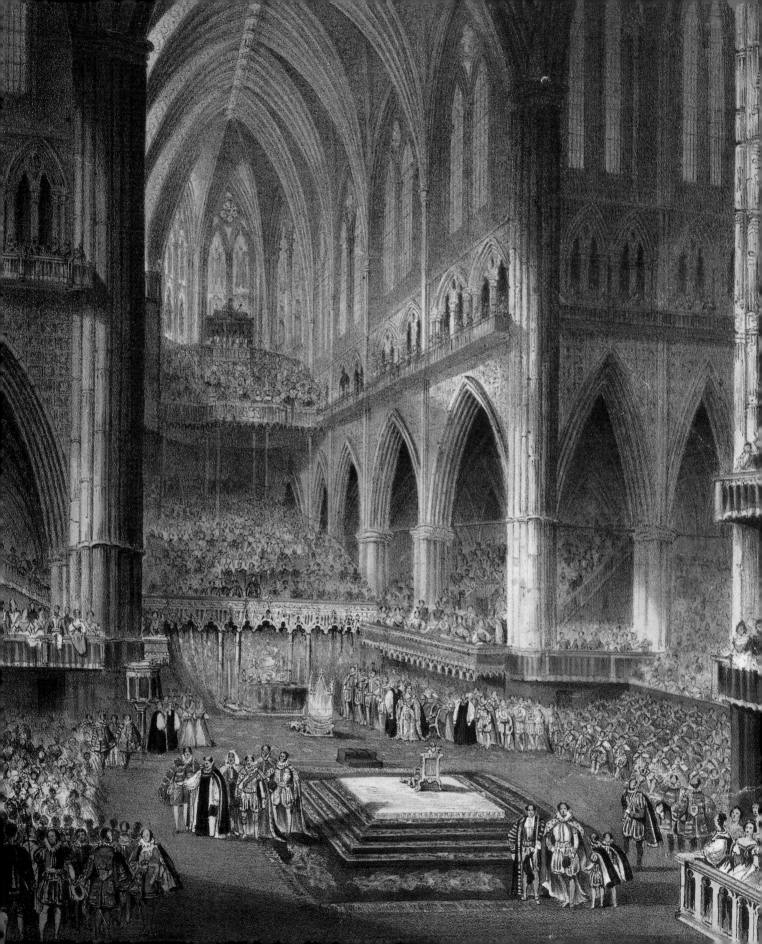

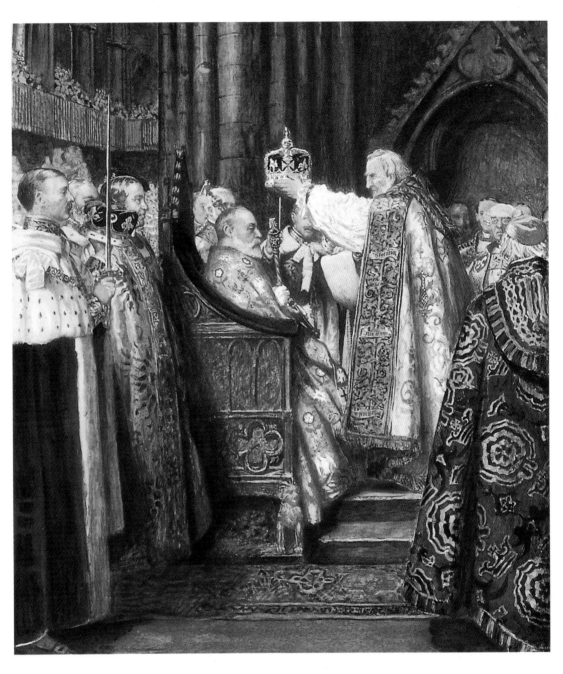

experience. One novelty was that the King allowed some still photographs to be taken inside the Abbey at the opening of the service.

On the day originally chosen for Edward VIII's coronation, it was his brother George VI who was crowned. The coronation in 1937 helped to heal the wounds caused by Edward VIII's abdication, as the new King and Queen convincingly demonstrated their regality. Though the King had a stammer, which made all public speaking difficult and the coronation oath a particular ordeal, he confounded those who had thought him a poor substitute for his more charismatic elder brother. It was not the King who faltered but some of his attendants, and more than once the King had to take control of proceedings. George VI had seen action with the Royal Navy during the First World War, and led the nation during the Second. Fittingly, his naval sword, presented to the Abbey by The Queen and The Queen Mother, commemorates this warrior-king in Westminster Abbey.

8 ELIZABETH II IS CROWNED

KING GEORGE VI died in his sleep during the early hours of 6 February 1952. On the death of a sovereign the crown passes instantly to the next in line. King George's elder daughter was 3,000 miles away in East Africa, watching wildlife from a treetop lodge, at the moment she became Queen Elizabeth II. Though the King had been seriously ill, his death at the age of fifty-six came with devastating suddenness. As soon as the difficult circumstances allowed, the new Queen flew back to London to take possession of her kingdom.

In earlier times a reign did not begin until the monarch was crowned. The principle of immediate succession was established in 1272 when Edward I was on crusade in the Holy Land at his father's death, and could not return to England for several years. Coronations were held as soon as possible, to confirm a regular succession or to validate an irregular one. Once sanctified with holy oil, a monarch could claim God's special protection against any opposition. As the political system became more settled and the constitutional monarchy evolved, the interval between accession and coronation lengthened. More time could be spent planning the ceremony, which became more lavish as a result. A summer's day could be chosen. Prolonged mourning for the previous sovereign could also be observed. All these factors contributed to the timing of Elizabeth II's coronation. It was already too late to plan for the summer of 1952, and the date was set for 2 June 1953.

The most time-consuming task was the transformation of the Abbey. Even though the structure of Henry III's church is designed with the coronation in mind, every occasion involves a major refit. This is arranged and paid for by the government, not the Abbey authorities. For a while some part of the church remained open for services; but from 1 January 1953 the Dean and Chapter had to surrender their keys to the Ministry of Works. It was the Minister, David (later Viscount) Eccles, who explained to journalists the guiding principles: 'The tradition and ceremony are inherited from the past and must be scrupulously preserved, but it is our duty to express in colour and design the age we live in and the Queen who is to be crowned.'

The achievement of these aims was to be a triumph. Within the Abbey itself the furnishings were of traditional design without being fussy. Lightweight modern materials and mass production helped to create a handsome temporary decor that did not detract from the dignity of the ancient surroundings. Elsewhere the visual style was that of the Festival of Britain, opened by George VI in 1951, blowing away the drabness of the post-war years with its refreshingly clean lines and bright colours.

The Abbey normally seats 2,200 people when full. For this coronation the capacity was increased to 8,000. Windows along both sides of the nave became doors, reached by raised walkways. To avoid the damage too often caused by preparations for earlier coronations, the floor was covered with felt and close-boarded, and all the monuments were boxed in. A railway track was laid from the west door to the lantern and the transepts to bring in hundreds of tons of scaffolding, seating and other materials. The infrastructure included a telephone exchange, control rooms, press facilities, powerful air conditioning and ten medical centres. The coronation stage was made by building the floor of the lantern up to the level of the sacrarium, with the throne raised five steps above it on a dais.

A large temporary annexe had to be built outside the west end of the Abbey. Here the processions were assembled and marshalled before they moved into the nave. Its other facilities included a dining room where The Queen and her closest family lunched after the service, before the long procession back through the streets of London to Buckingham Palace. The annexe had been needed since 1831, when William IV abandoned the banquet and the use of Westminster Hall. At first pseudo-Gothic pavilions were erected, but in 1937 and 1953 modern designs were preferred. It was also to the annexe that the regalia were carried by the Abbey clergy at the start of the ceremony, to be borne ahead of The Queen as she entered the church. For the rehearsals, replicas of the priceless ornaments had been made, and other sets were supplied for exhibitions. The real things arrived from the Tower of London only the night before, and for a few hours rested in Jerusalem Chamber under the eyes of the Yeomen Warders from the Tower.

The Ministry of Works had exhaustive negotiations with the suppliers of the equipment and furniture

OPPOSITE: This official coronation photograph of Elizabeth II by Cecil Beaton uses Henry VII's Chapel as the backdrop, though no part of the coronation ceremony takes place there.

ABOVE: Looking west along the nave during the six-month operation to prepare the Abbey for the coronation of Elizabeth II.

needed. There were, for example, to be 2,000 peers' chairs, each with the royal cypher embroidered on the back, and, mysteriously, 5,701 stools. Their padding had to be 12% cow-tail hair and 76% North American Grey Winter Hog. Precisely 2,287 yards of carpet were wanted, 13,000 yards of grey spun rayon for lining the walkways and hiding the scaffolding, 1,620 yards of damask for frontals and 17,700 yards of braid.

The Queen took a close interest in the furniture, which was to be newly made for her own use – the Chair of Estate, occupied at the start of the service, and the Throne for the homage. The Queen thought the Chair of Estate at her father's coronation had been 'too sumptuously upholstered for ceremonial duty'. On the other hand, Festival of Britain simplicity was not appropriate here. The Queen wanted the Chair of Estate and Throne to be dignified and splendid in appearance, and in keeping with their setting. Full-scale adjustable mock-ups were sent to Buckingham Palace and tested by The Queen in the robes she would be wearing. Both chairs were firmly

upholstered, and tailored to the most comfortable proportions. In the past there had been a footstool before the Throne. The Queen preferred to do without this, and the Throne was lowered five inches so that the royal feet could rest on the floor. The Queen also pointed out that a full version of her coat of arms embroidered on the chairs would not show up well from a distance. So instead the simpler and bolder emblem of the 'EIIR' cypher set within the Garter and surmounted by the crown was used.

Meanwhile there were extensive discussions about the exact form the service should take. Some felt that the ancient rite should be entirely revised, or that it should no longer be an exclusively Anglican affair. The Commonwealth had to be involved, for Elizabeth II would be crowned Queen not just of the United Kingdom but of its still vast empire and the independent dominions of Australia, Canada, Ceylon, New Zealand, Pakistan and South Africa. As Head of the Commonwealth she was the symbolic representative of 600 million people, a quarter of the world's population. The

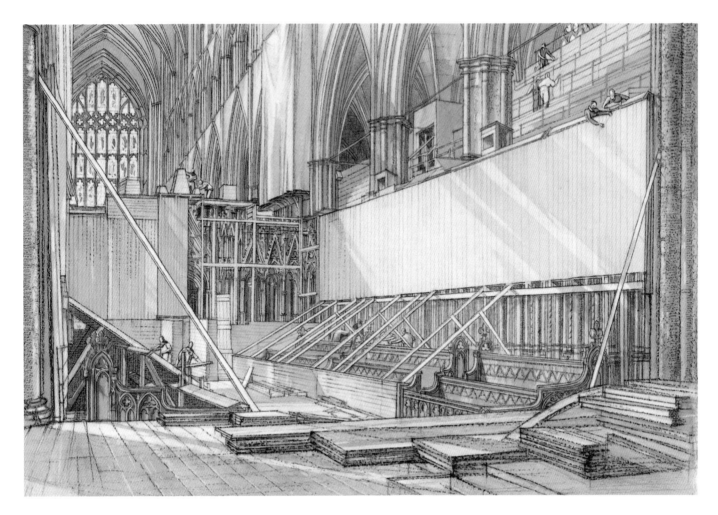

Duke of Edinburgh, who chaired the co-ordinating committee with his characteristic drive, was particularly keen to introduce features relevant to the modern world. There was a move to transform some of the secular ceremonial back to Westminster Hall. The Archbishop of Canterbury, Dr Geoffrey Fisher, talked out this idea, saying it would distract attention from the Abbey and the essentially religious nature of the day. In the end there were just a few carefully controlled innovations. The Moderator of the General Assembly of the Church of Scotland would present The Queen with a Bible. As the gift of the Commonwealth, a pair of gold bracelets was added to the regalia, reviving a feature not seen since the seventeenth century.

A new and difficult issue was whether the Abbey service should be televised, and if so how much of it. It was far from certain that the BBC's cameras would be allowed into the Abbey at all. Television was still in its infancy, reaching only a tiny proportion of households (about 1.5 million), and its equipment was cumbersome.

The Archbishop and the Dean of Westminster were apprehensive that any mistakes they made would be magnified, and both wanted no more than the processions to be shown. The Queen herself shared their concern. At first the Earl Marshal announced that, though film cameras would record the service, live television would show nothing east of the quire screen. The press erupted in fury, the *Daily Express* actually calling on The Queen 'to intercede and have a foolish deed undone'. Prime Minister Winston Churchill faced persistent questions in the House of Commons. The BBC then staged a mock broadcast, demonstrating that their technology could be unobtrusive and their presentation respectful. The Queen overcame her reservations, and the opposition gave way. The whole service would go out live on the BBC; but there were to be no close-up shots of The Queen, and some moments were still too sacred to be seen by the watching public. During the anointing the camera withdrew to a shot of the altar cross. Televising a communion service was novelty in

BELOW: The orb with the cross, carried in the monarch's left hand, is a symbolic reminder that the world is subject to 'the Power and Empire of Christ our Redeemer'.

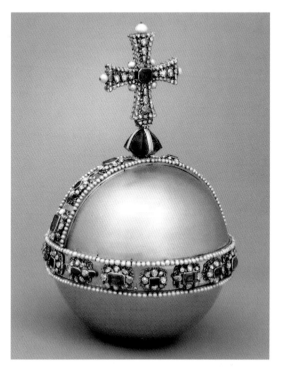

LEFT: After the coronation The Queen returned to Buckingham Palace by a long processional route. To avoid strain, the heavy golden orb was held in a bracket.

itself, and viewers neither saw nor heard the Archbishop consecrate the bread and wine. The taking of communion was also out of shot. These limitations upset nobody, and it was immediately apparent that a correct and portentous decision had been made.

Central to television's success was the role of the commentator Richard Dimbleby, who described the whole of the Abbey ceremony from a box high up in the triforium. Dimbleby was already an accomplished performer, but this was the biggest operation the BBC had yet mounted, and new skills had to be developed. The commentator had to know when to speak, for exactly how long and, more importantly, when to be silent. Dimbleby was particularly anxious that his voice should not cut across the words of the Archbishop or The Queen herself: 'This I think was the greatest strain, to speak at a critical moment, knowing that within a second or two something must happen over which one must not speak.' In the event Dimbleby's meticulous preparation and faultless delivery guided the watching nation expertly through the complexities of the ritual. Parts of the black-and-white television footage were incorporated in a colour film, which was distributed worldwide.

Many people bought a television set for the first time to watch the coronation broadcast. Most of them then found the flickering little screens hard to switch off, and the system grew significantly from that moment. Television had made the monarchy visible in an unprecedented way; and the monarchy lent respectability to the brash new medium. Though the two institutions have since then sometimes been at odds, a bond was forged through the great service in Westminster Abbey, and this has been reinforced every time the cameras have returned there to cover a royal occasion. One beneficial result is that ceremonies have been ever more carefully rehearsed, in the knowledge that mistakes would be preserved in film and videotape. At the 1953 coronation the only embarrassments were minor. The anointing takes place beneath a cloth of gold canopy supported by four Garter knights.

OPPOSITE: The Imperial State Crown as remodelled for The Queen. It was worn during the latter part of the coronation ceremony. It is also worn annually at the State Opening of Parliament.

As this was brought forward it brushed lightly against the central pinnacle of the Coronation Chair, where unfortunately a P.A. microphone had been too carefully hidden. One of the pages recalled the noise that echoed round the Abbey as 'rather like that of a hacksaw on lead.'

This blemish made no impact on the broadcast, since the BBC's microphones were taking only the crashing refrains of Handel's *Zadok the priest*. This anthem had been used during the anointing ever since its premiere at George II's coronation, and was an automatic choice. Parry's *I was glad* had also become a fixture, now adapted to incorporate *Vivat Regina Elizabetha*. There were six new musical commissions, including the beautiful little communion motet *O taste and see* written by Ralph Vaughan Williams. A novelty was the inclusion of a congregational hymn. The music committee was divided over the idea, but Fisher approved, and The Queen 'thought well of it',

so a hymn there was. Again it was Vaughan Williams who crafted a masterly arrangement of *All people that on earth do dwell*, embellishing the traditional 'Old Hundredth' tune with soaring trumpet descants.

The musical forces were commanded by the Abbey's Organist and Master of the Choristers, Dr (later Sir) William McKie. The appointment rested with the Earl Marshal and was not automatic; but McKie had impressed the authorities with his handling of the music for The Queen's wedding six years before. He was also an excellent administrator, an essential qualification since he had to organise a choir of 400 and an orchestra of eighty, brought together for this one occasion. McKie's advisers included his predecessor Sir Ernest Bullock, who directed the music at the 1937 coronation. Orchestral music played before the service was conducted by Sir Adrian Boult.

ABOVE: The Queen, moments after receiving St Edward's Crown, holds the Rod 'of equity and mercy' and the Sceptre, 'the ensign of kingly power and justice'.

AS AN ELEVEN-YEAR-OLD at Westminster Abbey Choir School I sang at the coronation, and I have vivid memories of that day. We had been anticipating it for more than fifteen months, since we first saw the union flag on Victoria Tower being lowered to half mast on 6 February 1952, and heard the Abbey's tenor bell tolling once each minute. A member of staff interrupted our Latin lesson to tell us the King had died. Regrettably, our sorrow at the news was quickly overtaken by our excitement at the thought of new stamps and coins with The Queen's head on them, then by further excitement at the thought of a coronation in which we would take part. With the Abbey closed for its interior to be transformed, we began rehearsing the music. One piece, the *Te Deum* by William Walton, with its syncopated rhythms, was particularly tricky to learn. Walton himself rehearsed it with us. The night before the coronation, after a pillow fight in the dormitory, we did not sleep well and were up at dawn to watch the activity below us in Dean's Yard. After breakfast, and a brief rehearsal in the Song School to tune up our voices, we processed through the cloisters into the Abbey. At the dress rehearsal we had been astonished on entering the Abbey to see not the familiar pillars and long vistas but scaffolding, plywood walls, stairways, direction signs and fire extinguishers; but it was only on the day itself, when we emerged onto the coronation theatre, that we got the first breathtaking view of the Abbey in its finery. Bathed in powerful television lights, the setting seemed to sparkle all the more. We processed to the high altar and waited while the Abbey clergy collected the regalia. Then, together, we processed through the Abbey,

singing the Litany, to the annexe, where the regalia was placed on an altar-like side table so it could be later carried back through the Abbey in The Queen's procession.

Once in our places, in the front two rows of the specially built stands above the south quire aisle, we took in more fully the glorious riot of colour – the vivid ermine-trimmed crimson robes of the peers and peeresses, the blue and gold carpets and, in the quire, the VIPs, among them ambassadors, princes from Ethiopia, Laos, Vietnam, Cambodia and Thailand, the rulers of Kuwait and Bahrain, and the Sultans of Zanzibar and Perak, many arrayed in gorgeous uniforms with shimmering jewels. Just below us was the Queen of Tonga who had endeared herself to the public by riding in an open-topped carriage despite the rain. With two hours to wait until the service started we prematurely ate our picnic lunch of ham sandwiches and apples, which had been provided in our cassock pockets. The bench seating was very cramped, and our only option for stretching our legs was over the laps of our neighbours, undignified but very necessary as the hours ticked by. Just before the service there was increased excitement and everyone stood, thinking The Queen had arrived. Instead, from under the organ loft came four cleaners armed with carpet sweepers for a last minute tidy up. To a burst of laughter everyone sat down again. Eventually, with The Queen processing slowly up the nave, we began the opening anthem, Parry's *I was glad*. William McKie later said that as soon as the first notes had been sung he knew that the service would go well. The Queen was led to all four sides of the theatre and presented to the congregation for the Recognition. We were asked whether we were willing to do our homage. According to the Order of Service the congregation were to 'signify their willingness and joy by loud and repeated acclamations, all with one voice crying out "God Save Queen Elizabeth"' – the only time an Abbey congregation is encouraged to shout. Shout we all did, but I was disappointed that everyone shouted in unison; I had expected a cheer of approval as one might hear at a football match when a goal is scored.

The music during the service went well, and when it was over the choir was one of the first groups to be released. Back at the Choir School we had a special tea of boiled eggs, quite a treat as we normally only had bread and butter.

JAMES WILKINSON, CO-AUTHOR

9 CHURCH, CROWN AND COMMONWEALTH

I N THE LAST 100 YEARS Westminster Abbey has hosted an increasing number and variety of royal occasions. Indeed the links between 'Crown and Cloister' have never been stronger. The present Queen does not worship in the Abbey on a daily basis, as some of her ancestors did, but in the course of her reign she has attended numerous services and social events. Other members of the Royal Family are frequent visitors, often as patrons of particular organisations. There have also been many times when the whole Royal Family has been present, sharing their joys and sorrows with the nation and the Commonwealth.

Royal weddings feature little in the Abbey's story until the twentieth century; before this only two reigning monarchs have ever married there – Richard II and Henry VII. The first of the modern weddings was that of Princess Patricia of Connaught, a granddaughter of Queen Victoria, in 1919. Four years later, George V's second son, the Duke of York, married Lady Elizabeth Bowes-Lyon, a

union that was to have greater significance than could be foreseen at the time. The wedding in 1934 of George V's fourth son, the Duke of Kent, to Princess Marina of Greece, was the first royal occasion to be broadcast (on radio) from the Abbey. The present Queen, as Princess Elizabeth, married the former Prince Philip of Greece in November 1947, when royal pageantry was resumed after the Second World War. It was still a time of austerity, and the bride's dress had to be bought with the permitted ration coupons. The groom, having renounced his Greek titles on becoming a British citizen, was on the eve of his wedding created Duke of Edinburgh, a Royal Highness and a Knight of the Garter. It was, as George VI told his mother, 'a great deal to give a man all at once'. Prince Philip has gone on to fulfil countless functions for the monarchy. One of them was to give away his sister-in-law, Princess Margaret, at her Abbey wedding in 1960. The Queen's cousin, Princess Alexandra, was married in the Abbey in 1963. The Queen and Prince Philip cele-

OPPOSITE: The Queen, preceded by The Prince of Wales as Great Master of the Order, at an installation service for Knights Grand Cross of the Bath in 2006.

RIGHT: The Queen talking to some of those who have taken part in the annual Commonwealth Observance.

brated their silver wedding with an Abbey service in 1972, and would return to mark their gold and diamond anniversaries. Meanwhile the weddings of their children Princess Anne (1973) and the Duke of York (1986) had also taken place in the Abbey.

The installation services for the Order of the Bath, which had been abandoned in 1847, were revived in the reign of George V. Though the outdoor procession was soon dropped, making the plumed hats shown by Canaletto redundant, it is still the greatest spectacle seen at the Abbey apart from a coronation. The services are normally held every four years, and alternate installations are usually graced by the presence of The Queen. A major part is played by The Prince of Wales, who since 1973 has been Great Master of the Order. In 1815 the Order was remodelled with three grades, of which only the highest, Knights (and, since 1971 Dames) Grand Cross, wear the full insignia and are installed. There are not enough stalls for them all in Henry VII's Chapel, and GCBs may wait many years for installation. An honorary GCB is also The Queen's usual gift to a visiting head of state. American Presidents may not receive foreign honours while in office, but General Eisenhower already had the order, and it was given in retirement to Ronald Reagan and George Bush senior.

Also associated with the Abbey is the 'Office of the Royal Maundy', when, each year on the day before Good Friday, token alms are distributed to a select body of old people, as many of each sex as the monarch has years of age. The coins given include the specially minted Maundy pieces. The ceremony was originally incidental to a ritual washing of feet, commemorating the humble act performed by Christ at the Last Supper, still part of the Maundy Thursday liturgy in some churches. In fact, the Royal Maundy was held regularly at the Abbey only between 1890 and 1952. During the present reign it has increasingly been taken to cathedrals and other great churches around the country, and now returns to the Abbey every tenth year. It was, however, during its 'Abbey period' that the service acquired much of its present character, of which several elements were devised by the then Abbey librarian, Lawrence Tanner, who was also secretary of the Royal Almonry. The most important development came in 1932 when King George V attended and distributed the Maundy coins, as no monarch had done in person since 1698. This set a precedent that, with the advent of social welfare, has fortuitously made the Maundy service a cherished symbol of the caring role of the State.

The Commonwealth Day Observance in March is an annual occasion, which brings The Queen to Westminster Abbey. This colourful and vibrant act of dedication brings together people of different faiths in a format beyond the possibilities of a Christian service, however liberal. There is a Christian orientation appropriate to the Abbey as host, but the emphasis is on beliefs and values affirmed by all faiths: the unique worth and dignity of each individual, justice for all, peace between nations and respect for the environment. The Abbey resounds with music more diverse and more lively than is customary, and observes the Biblical recommendation that there is a time to dance.

The Royal Family's connection with the Abbey is by no means purely ceremonial. Although appointments to the Chapter are made on the recommendation of the Prime Minister, this is an area in which The Queen is known to be closely concerned. Prince Philip has had an active role as president of the Westminster Abbey Trust, which successfully raised £25 million needed for the restoration of the exterior fabric. To mark the completion of this work in 1995, The Queen unveiled a stained-glass window in Henry VII's Chapel.

At the start of the twentieth century considerations of space and growing public acceptance of cremation led to a decision to restrict Abbey burials to the interment of ashes. One important exception was the burial in 1920 of the body of a soldier of the First World War, unknown by name or rank, as a symbolic representative of the British war dead. The Grave of the Unknown Warrior gave a new dimension to the Abbey's status as the national mausoleum, and set a precedent adopted in many countries. The idea came from an army chaplain, and it was keenly promoted by the Dean of Westminster, Herbert Ryle. King George V at first rejected what he felt might be thought a 'belated' gesture, perhaps also with royalty's instinctive suspicion of designed effect. Once his misgiv-

ings had been resolved, the King agreed to attend the funeral, which was to follow the unveiling of the Cenotaph in Whitehall on Armistice Day, 11 November. So the King walked behind the gun carriage on which was borne to Westminster Abbey one of the one million of his subjects who had given their lives for God, King and country.

The First World War was fondly expected to end all further violence in the name of politics. The futility of that hope is adequately stated in a floor-stone next to the Grave of the Unknown Warrior, which bids us 'Remember Winston Churchill'. This memorial was unveiled by The Queen in 1965, a few months after Churchill's death. Close by is remembered Prince Philip's uncle, Earl Mountbatten of Burma, killed by a terrorist bomb in 1979. It had long been intended that Lord Mountbatten's unique and illustrious career should be marked by a funeral of special solemnity in the Abbey, and Mountbatten had devised the details with military precision. Everything was done as he had wanted, though the circumstances of his death gave the service an especially sombre character.

The Prince of Wales had a special affection for Lord Mountbatten, whom he called his 'honorary grandfather', and he read the lesson at the funeral. It is said that the memory of this painful occasion prompted him to choose St Paul's Cathedral for his wedding two years later to Lady Diana Spencer. That marriage ended in the divorce courts in 1991, but its final drama was to be played out in Westminster Abbey.

At 6.30 on the morning of Sunday 31 August 1997 the Dean of Westminster was woken by a telephone call with the news that Diana, Princess of Wales, had died a few hours earlier after a road accident in Paris. Later in the day he was informed that The Queen had ordered an Abbey funeral for the Princess. Preparations had to begin at once and from scratch because the circumstances were without precedent. They were also fraught with awkwardness because of the need to respect the divergent concerns of the Royal Family and the Spencer family, and to respond in some measure to mounting public grief, which developed rapidly and almost reached mass hysteria. As soon as the first arrangements for the funeral were announced, the railings of the

Abbey became festooned with flowers, and hundreds began to camp outside to await events. Although the Princess had technically lost her royal status, she had remained a charismatic celebrity, and the sudden horror of her death seemed to add the crown of martyrdom. It was difficult to decide what form of service would be appropriate. The Abbey was deluged with well-meaning and impractical suggestions; but it was recognised that something other than conventional church music would be needed to represent popular feeling. As a result the singer and songwriter Elton John was invited to take part. In the event his restrained performance at the piano was upstaged by the Princess's brother, Earl Spencer, whose eulogy attracted both strident applause from some quarters and outrage from others.

The former Princess of Wales's funeral was easily the most witnessed occasion in the Abbey's history; indeed it is said to have had the largest ever television audience for any single event – some two billion viewers worldwide. Most observers were appreciative, and the faultless execution of the hastily contrived service enhanced the Abbey's reputation for musical and ceremonial excellence.

Queen Elizabeth The Queen Mother once told Edward Carpenter, a former Dean of Westminster, that all the most significant occasions of her life had taken place at the Abbey – her wedding, her coronation, the weddings of her two daughters and her elder daughter's coronation. Conventionally, dowager queens do not attend subsequent coronations; but after the trauma of the abdication Queen Mary had been determined to see her son George VI crowned, and that precedent was happily followed by her daughter-in-law in 1953. Queen Elizabeth was a frequent visitor to the Abbey throughout almost seventy years of public service. Twice she distributed the Maundy money on behalf of The Queen. Every year she visited the Garden of Remembrance, a field of poppies laid out on the Abbey's north green to mark Armistice Day, and laid her own small cross in tribute to the war dead. The formal timetable was invariably disregarded as Queen Elizabeth talked at length to ex-servicemen and -women, with whom she shared so many memories.

There were lighter moments, too. Queen Elizabeth was entertained by the Dean and Chapter in the Jerusalem Chamber when she celebrated her eightieth birthday in 1980. As he proposed the toast, Dean Carpenter accidentally took Queen Elizabeth's glass, so that she was unable to accept his invitation to share the moment: 'I'd love to, Mr Dean', she said, 'but you've nicked my drink'. Ten years later another landmark birthday was marked by another Abbey party; the choristers sang Scottish airs, which reduced her private secretary to tears, and the Queen Mother spoke of her love for 'this holy place'.

It was, therefore, altogether fitting that when Queen Elizabeth's life finally closed at the age of 101 her funeral, by her own request, took place in the Abbey. A precedent had been established with the Abbey funeral of Queen Alexandra, widow of Edward VII, in 1925, which had revived a tradition dating back to the funeral of Queen Edith, widow of the Confessor himself, in 1075.

Despite her great age, the Queen Mother's death on Easter Eve 2002 still came as a shock. Thirty minutes before the public announcement the news was given to the Abbey, where extensive preparations were already being made for a memorial service to Princess Margaret, who had died on 9 February. The Queen Mother had last been seen in public when she attended her younger daughter's funeral at Windsor. This double bereavement threatened to blight the imminent celebration of The Queen's Golden Jubilee. Yet these successive events showed once again the representative potency of the hereditary monarchy, one family whose living and dying touches the whole nation.

For several days before her funeral the Queen Mother's body lay in state in Westminster Hall, her glittering personal crown resting above the coffin. As was customary, the Abbey's processional cross and candlesticks surrounded the catafalque, and the men of the Abbey choir sang as the coffin was borne into the Hall, emphasising that this was not only a state occasion but also the start of a Christian funeral. On 9 April the body was then taken the short distance across Parliament Square to the Abbey for the funeral service. On this familiar stage one of the most cherished figures in the monarchy's long history was saluted for the last time.

ABOVE: Queen Elizabeth The Queen Mother, regularly opened the Field of Remembrance outside the Abbey, where the dead of two world wars and more recent conflicts are annually honoured.

The Dean of Westminster concludes:

This inspiring story of intertwined history between 'Crown and Cloister' continues. The daily life of Westminster Abbey, as a Royal Peculiar, remains closely linked to the monarchy. The Queen and members of the Royal Family attend on a regular basis many of the Abbey's national services, which commemorate important events or anniversaries in the life of the country. The Abbey's bells ring out regularly to celebrate the birthdays of members of the Royal Family. Each year the Abbey submits an account of its activities to The Queen, who continues to take a close and personal interest in all its work. The story sketched in this book is as real and continuing today as it has ever been.

The life of the Abbey moves on. Rich as its history has continually been in the story of the nation over the last thousand years, the Abbey is not a museum to the past but a living church, which goes continually forward and plans for the future. It does so within the context of the 450th anniversary in 2010 of the charter granted to the Abbey by Queen Elizabeth I, which continues to inspire the commitment of this 1,000-year-old Abbey to the service of God and its mission to the Crown, the State and the nation – a mission in which the Abbey takes great and lasting pride.

THE ROYAL FAMILY TREE SHOWING THE DESCENT OF THE CROWN

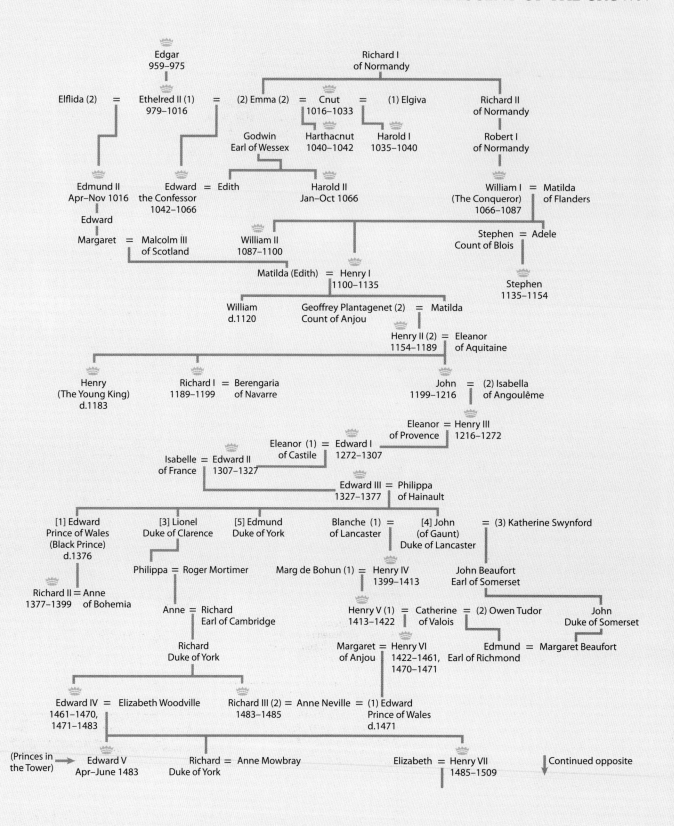

Edgar
959–975

Richard I
of Normandy

Elflida (2) = Ethelred II (1)
979–1016

(2) Emma (2) = Cnut
1016–1033

= (1) Elgiva

Richard II
of Normandy

Godwin
Earl of Wessex

Harthacnut
1040–1042

Harold I
1035–1040

Robert I
of Normandy

Edmund II
Apr–Nov 1016

Edward
the Confessor
1042–1066

= Edith

Harold II
Jan–Oct 1066

William I
(The Conqueror)
1066–1087

= Matilda
of Flanders

Edward

Margaret = Malcolm III
of Scotland

William II
1087–1100

Stephen = Adele
Count of Blois

Matilda (Edith) = Henry I
1100–1135

Stephen
1135–1154

William
d.1120

Geoffrey Plantagenet (2) = Matilda
Count of Anjou

Henry II (2) = Eleanor
1154–1189   of Aquitaine

Henry
(The Young King)
d.1183

Richard I = Berengaria
1189–1199   of Navarre

John = (2) Isabella
1199–1216   of Angoulême

Eleanor = Henry III
of Provence 1216–1272

Eleanor (1) = Edward I
of Castile   1272–1307

Isabelle = Edward II
of France   1307–1327

Edward III = Philippa
1327–1377   of Hainault

[1] Edward
Prince of Wales
(Black Prince)
d.1376

[3] Lionel
Duke of Clarence

[5] Edmund
Duke of York

Blanche (1) =
of Lancaster

[4] John
(of Gaunt)
Duke of Lancaster

= (3) Katherine Swynford

Philippa = Roger Mortimer

Marg de Bohun (1) = Henry IV
1399–1413

John Beaufort
Earl of Somerset

Richard II = Anne
1377–1399   of Bohemia

Anne = Richard
Earl of Cambridge

Henry V (1) = Catherine = (2) Owen Tudor
1413–1422   of Valois

John
Duke of Somerset

Richard
Duke of York

Margaret = Henry VI
of Anjou   1422–1461,
1470–1471

Edmund = Margaret Beaufort
Earl of Richmond

Edward IV = Elizabeth Woodville
1461–1470,
1471–1483

Richard III (2) = Anne Neville = (1) Edward
1483–1485   Prince of Wales
d.1471

(Princes in
the Tower) → Edward V
Apr–June 1483

Richard = Anne Mowbray
Duke of York

Elizabeth = Henry VII
1485–1509

Continued opposite

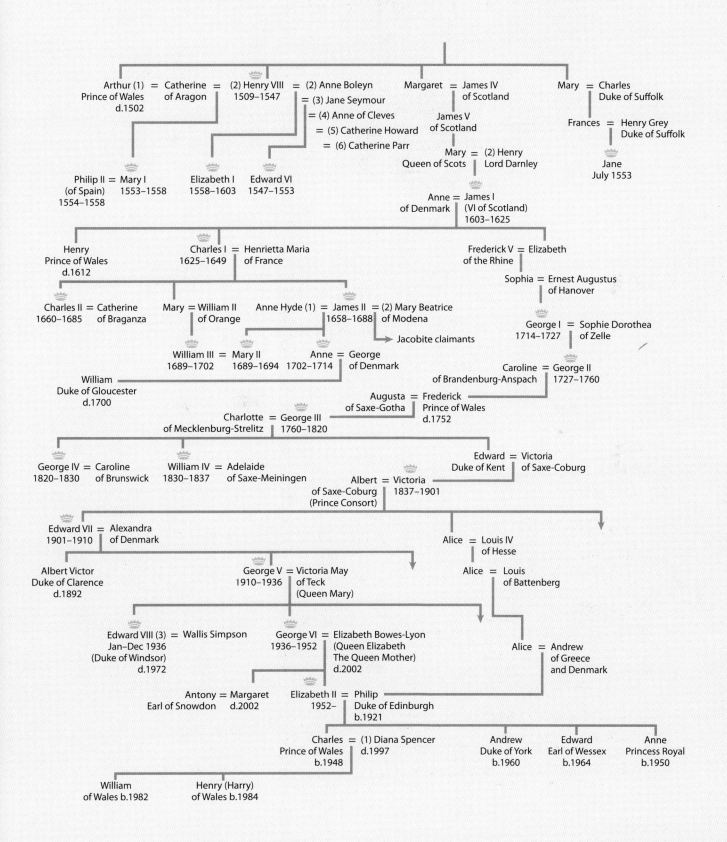

Arthur (1) = Catherine = (2) Henry VIII = (2) Anne Boleyn
Prince of Wales   of Aragon   1509–1547
d.1502
                              = (3) Jane Seymour
                              = (4) Anne of Cleves
                                  = (5) Catherine Howard
                                  = (6) Catherine Parr

Margaret = James IV
              of Scotland

James V
of Scotland

Mary = (2) Henry
Queen of Scots   Lord Darnley

Mary = Charles
          Duke of Suffolk

Frances = Henry Grey
              Duke of Suffolk

Jane
July 1553

Philip II = Mary I
(of Spain)   1553–1558
1554–1558

Elizabeth I
1558–1603

Edward VI
1547–1553

Anne = James I
of Denmark   (VI of Scotland)
              1603–1625

Henry
Prince of Wales
d.1612

Charles I = Henrietta Maria
1625–1649   of France

Frederick V = Elizabeth
                  of the Rhine

Sophia = Ernest Augustus
              of Hanover

Charles II = Catherine
1660–1685   of Braganza

Mary = William II
          of Orange

Anne Hyde (1) = James II = (2) Mary Beatrice
                  1658–1688   of Modena

→ Jacobite claimants

George I = Sophie Dorothea
1714–1727   of Zelle

William III = Mary II
1689–1702   1689–1694

Anne = George
1702–1714   of Denmark

William
Duke of Gloucester
d.1700

Caroline = George II
of Brandenburg-Anspach   1727–1760

Augusta = Frederick
of Saxe-Gotha   Prince of Wales
                  d.1752

Charlotte = George III
of Mecklenburg-Strelitz   1760–1820

George IV = Caroline
1820–1830   of Brunswick

William IV = Adelaide
1830–1837   of Saxe-Meiningen

Edward = Victoria
Duke of Kent   of Saxe-Coburg

Albert = Victoria
of Saxe-Coburg   1837–1901
(Prince Consort)

Edward VII = Alexandra
1901–1910   of Denmark

Alice = Louis IV
          of Hesse

Albert Victor
Duke of Clarence
d.1892

George V = Victoria May
1910–1936   of Teck
              (Queen Mary)

Alice = Louis
          of Battenberg

Edward VIII (3) = Wallis Simpson
Jan–Dec 1936
(Duke of Windsor)
d.1972

George VI = Elizabeth Bowes-Lyon
1936–1952   (Queen Elizabeth
              The Queen Mother)
              d.2002

Alice = Andrew
          of Greece
          and Denmark

Antony = Margaret
Earl of Snowdon   d.2002

Elizabeth II = Philip
1952–   Duke of Edinburgh
              b.1921

Charles = (1) Diana Spencer
Prince of Wales   d.1997
b.1948

Andrew
Duke of York
b.1960

Edward
Earl of Wessex
b.1964

Anne
Princess Royal
b.1950

William
of Wales b.1982

Henry (Harry)
of Wales b.1984

KINGS AND QUEENS OF ENGLAND SINCE 1042, OF GREAT BRITAIN SINCE 1603

	EFFECTIVE REIGN	CROWNED	DIED	LAST BURIAL PLACE (* SURVIVING EFFIGY ON TOMB)
HOUSE OF WESSEX				
Edward the Confessor	1042–1066	1043	1066	Westminster Abbey
Harold II	1066	1066	1066	? Waltham Abbey
HOUSE OF NORMANDY				
William I	1066–1087	1066	1087	St Stephen's Abbey, Caen
William II	1087–1100	1087	1100	Winchester Cathedral
Henry I	1100–1135	1100	1135	Reading Abbey
Stephen	1135–1154	1135	1154	Faversham Abbey
HOUSE OF ANJOU				
Henry II	1154–1189	1154	1189	Fontevrault Abbey*
Richard I	1189–1199	1189	1199	Fontevrault Abbey*
John	1199–1216	1199	1216	Worcester Cathedral*
Henry III	1216–1272	1216	1272	Westminster Abbey*
Edward I	1272–1307	1274	1307	Westminster Abbey
Edward II	1307–1327	1308	1327	Gloucester Cathedral*
Edward III	1327–1377	1327	1377	Westminster Abbey*
Richard II	1377–1399	1377	1400	Westminster Abbey*
HOUSE OF LANCASTER				
Henry IV	1399–1413	1399	1413	Canterbury Cathedral*
Henry V	1413–1422	1413	1422	Westminster Abbey*
Henry VI	1422–1460	1429		
restored	1470–1471		1471	St George's Chapel, Windsor
HOUSE OF YORK				
Edward IV	1461–1470	1461		
restored	1471–1483		1483	St George's Chapel, Windsor
Edward V	1483		?1485	? Westminster Abbey
Richard III	1483–1485	1485	1485	Greyfriars, Leicester
HOUSE OF TUDOR				
Henry VII	1485–1509	1485	1509	Westminster Abbey*
Henry VIII	1509–1547	1509	1609	St George's Chapel, Windsor
Edward VI	1547–1553	1547	1553	Westminster Abbey
Jane	1553		1554	Tower of London
Mary I	1553–1558	1553	1558	Westminster Abbey
Elizabeth I	1558–1603	1559	1603	Westminster Abbey*
HOUSE OF STUART				
James I	1603–1625	1603	1625	Westminster Abbey
Charles I	1625–1649	1626	1649	St George's Chapel, Windsor

Republic				
Charles II	1660–1685	1661	1685	Westminster Abbey
James II	1685–1688	1685	1701	Church of St Germain en Laye
Interregnum				
William III	1689–1702	1689	1702	Westminster Abbey
& Mary II	1689–1694	1689	1694	Westminster Abbey
Anne	1702–1714	1702	1714	Westminster Abbey

HOUSE OF HANOVER

George I	1714–1727	1714	1727	Herrenhausen Gardens, Hanover
George II	1727–1760	1727	1760	Westminster Abbey
George III	1760–1820	1761	1820	St George's Chapel, Windsor
George IV	1820–1830	1821	1830	St George's Chapel, Windsor
William IV	1830–1837	1831	1837	St George's Chapel, Windsor
Victoria	1837–1901	1838	1901	Frogmore Mausoleum, Windsor*

HOUSE OF SAXE-COBURG

Edward VII	1901–1910	1902	1910	St George's Chapel, Windsor*

HOUSE OF WINDSOR

George V	1910–1936	1911	1936	St George's Chapel, Windsor*
Edward VIII	1936		1972	Frogmore Mausoleum, Windsor
George VI	1936–1952	1937	1952	St George's Chapel, Windsor
Elizabeth II	1952–	1953		

All monarchs since William I (probably also his predecessor Harold) have been crowned in Westminster Abbey, except Edward V and Edward VIII, whose reigns ended before coronation could take place. Henry III was first crowned Gloucester Cathedral, and was crowned again in Westminster Abbey in 1220.

HEIR APPARENT CROWNED IN WESTMINSTER ABBEY:

Henry, son of Henry II (1170)

CONSORTS CROWNED WITH THEIR HUSBANDS IN WESTMINSTER ABBEY:

Eleanor of Aquitaine, with Henry II (1154)
Eleanor of Castile, with Edward I (1274)
Isabelle of France, with Edward II (1308)
Anne Neville, with Richard III (1485)
Catherine of Aragon, with Henry VIII (1509)
Anne of Denmark, with James I (1603)
Mary Beatrice of Modena, with James II (1685)
Caroline of Brandeburg-Anspach, with George II (1727)
Charlotte of Mecklenburg-Strelitz, with George III (1761)
Adelaide of Saxe-Meiningen, with William IV (1831)
Alexandra of Denmark, with Edward VII (1902)
Mary of Teck, with George V (1911)
Elizabeth Bowes-Lyon, with George VI (1937)

CONSORTS CROWNED SEPARATELY IN WESTMINSTER ABBEY:

Matilda of Flanders, wife of William I (1068)
Matilda of Scotland, first wife of Henry I (1100)
Adeliza of Lorraine, second wife of Henry I (1121)
Matilda of Boulogne, wife of Stephen (1136)
Isabella of Angoulême, second wife of John (1200)
Eleanor of Provence, wife of Henry III (1236)
Philippa of Hainault, wife of Edward III (1328)
Anne of Bohemia, first wife of Richard II (1382)
Isabelle of France, second wife of Richard II (1397)
Joan of Navarre, second wife of Henry IV (1403)
Catherine of Valois, wife of Henry V (1421)
Margaret of Anjou, wife of Henry VI (1445)
Elizabeth Woodville, wife of Edward IV (1465)
Elizabeth of York, wife of Henry VII (1487)
Anne Boleyn, second wife of Henry VIII (1533)

MONARCHS MARRIED IN WESTMINSTER ABBEY:

Richard II (1382)
Henry VII (1486)
George VI (1923, when Duke of York)
Elizabeth II (1947, when Princess Elizabeth)

For a comprehensive account of the complexities and uncertainties of some of the burials see A. Dodson *The Royal Tombs of Great Britain: An Illustrated History* (London, 2004)

INDEX

Note: Page numbers in *italics* indicate illustrations.

© Scala Publishers Ltd, 2010
Text © James Wilkinson and C.S. Knighton, 2010
Photography © Dean and Chapter of Westminster, 2010,
(pp. 4, 34 by David Lambert), except:

back cover (paperback), inside cover (paperback), endpapers
(hardback), pp. 43 (left), 46, 55 © Bridgeman Art Library
p. 12 (top) © Reproduced by kind permission of the Syndics
of Cambridge University Library
pp. 68, 81 © Corbis
p. 26 (top) © Derek Chivers
pp. 77, 78 © Getty Images
pp. 70, 71 © Sir Henry Rushbury / John Mowlem
front cover (paperback), cover (hardback), pp. 1, 72 (left), 73
The Royal Collection © 2010 Her Majesty Queen Elizabeth II
p. 75 © James Wilkinson
p. 13 © J.G. O'Neilly
pp. 2, 12 (bottom), 18–19, 35, 36 (left), 49, 53 © Malcolm
Crowthers
pp. 37 (right), 43 (right), 45 © National Portrait Gallery
p. 36 (right) © Queens' College, Cambridge
p. 37 (left) © Society of Antiquaries of London
pp. 51, 72 (right), 74 © Woodmansterne Publications Ltd
p. 42 © Worshipful Company of Barber Surgeons

First published in 2010 by
Scala Publishers Ltd
Northburgh House
10 Northburgh St
London EC1V 0AT
Telephone: +44 (0) 20 7490 9900
www.scalapublishers.com

Hardback: ISBN-13: 978 1 85759 630 4
Paperback: ISBN-13: 978 1 85759 628 1

Text: James Wilkinson and C.S. Knighton
Editor: Esme West
Designer: Nigel Soper
Printed and bound in China

10 9 8 7 6 5 4 3 2 1

British Library Cataloguing in Publication Data
A catalogue record for this book is available from
the British Library.

Cover (hardback), front cover (paperback): The coronation of
Queen Victoria in 1838, illustrated by Sir George Hayter, 1839,
from the Royal Collection
Back cover (paperback): Detail of the 'Armada' portrait of
Elizabeth I, c.1588, by George Gower, from the collection of
Woburn Abbey
Inside cover (paperback), endpapers (hardback): View of
Parliament, showing the west towers of Westminster Abbey
beyond, by George Fennel Robson, nineteenth century
Page 1: St Edward's Crown, part of the coronation regalia, from
the Royal Collection
Page 2: One of the gilded lions supporting the Coronation Chair
Page 4: View of the quire at Westminster Abbey looking east